CAMPAIGN • 210

OPERATION *DRAGOON* 1944

France's other D-Day

STEVEN J ZALOGA

ILLUSTRATED BY JOHN WHITE
Series editors Marcus Cowper and Nikolai Bogdanovic

First published in Great Britain in 2009 by Osprey Publishing,
Midland House, West Way, Botley, Oxford OX2 0PH, UK
44-02 23rd St, Suite 219, Long Island City, NY 11101, USA
Email: info@ospreypublishing.com

© 2009 Osprey Publishing Ltd

A CIP catalog record for this book is available from the British Library.

ISBN: 978 1 84603 367 4
PDF e-book ISBN: 978 1 84603 898 3

Editorial by Ilios Publishing Ltd, Oxford, UK (www.iliospublishing.com)
Page layout by The Black Spot
Index by Glyn Sutcliffe
Typeset in Sabon and Myriad Pro
Maps by Bounford.com
3D bird's-eye views by The Black Spot
Battlescene illustrations by John White
Originated by PPS Grasmere Ltd
Printed in China through Worldprint

10 11 12 13 14   12 11 10 9 8 7 6 5 4 3

ARTIST'S NOTE

Readers may care to note that the original paintings from which the
color plates in this book were prepared are available for private sale.
All reproduction copyright whatsoever is retained by the Publishers.
All enquiries should be addressed to:

John White
5107 C Monroe Road
Charlotte
NC 28205
USA

The Publishers regret that they can enter into no correspondence upon
this matter.

THE WOODLAND TRUST

Osprey Publishing are supporting the Woodland Trust, the UK's leading
woodland conservation charity, by funding the dedication of trees.

Key to military symbols

Army Group	Army	Corps	Division	Brigade	Regiment	Battalion
Company/Battery	Platoon	Section	Squad	Infantry	Artillery	Cavalry
Airborne	Unit HQ	Air defense	Air Force	Air mobile	Air transportable	Amphibious
Antitank	Armor	Air aviation	Bridging	Engineer	Headquarters	Maintenance
Medical	Missile	Mountain	Navy	Nuclear, biological, chemical	Ordnance	Parachute
Reconnaissance	Signal	Supply	Transport movement	Rocket artillery	Air defense artillery	

Key to unit identification

Unit identifier | Parent unit
Commander
(+) with added elements
(−) less elements

CONTENTS

German Army tactical and occupation units, Mediterranean coast, August 1944

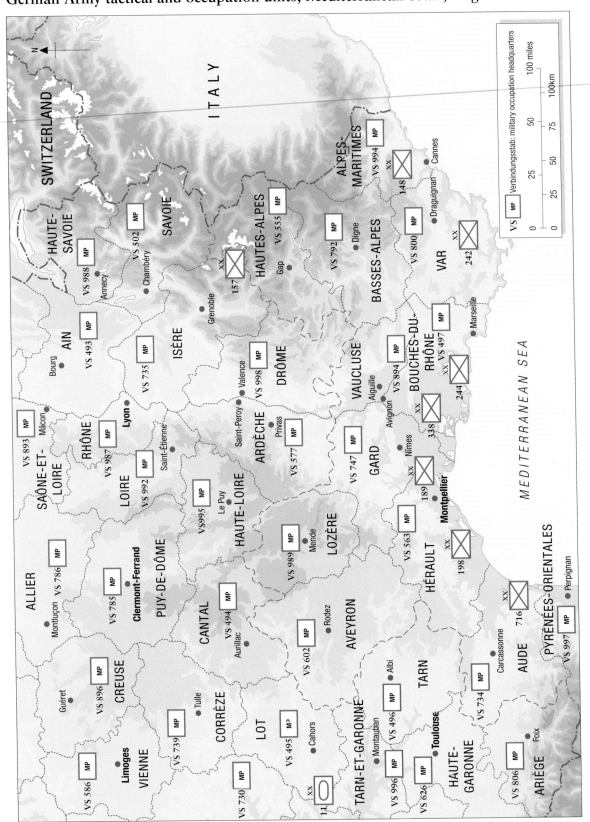

INTRODUCTION

The invasion of southern France on August 15, 1944, is one of the least celebrated yet most important combat operations by the Allies in the summer of 1944. Originating in a bitter strategic dispute between senior US and British leaders, Operation *Dragoon* succeeded far beyond the wildest dreams of its advocates. The Wehrmacht's Heeresgruppe G in southern and central France, weakened by diversions of its meager forces to Italy and Normandy, was unable to create a viable defense and so was forced to withdraw. Instead of a bitter battle of attrition akin to Anzio or Normandy, *Dragoon* quickly turned into a headlong retreat by German forces up the Rhône Valley with American and French troops in hot pursuit. In the process of retreat,

The driving force behind Operation *Dragoon* was the US Army Chief of Staff, General George C. Marshall. He did not favor the continued diversion of US forces to the Mediterranean theater after the fall of Rome in June 1944. Furthermore, Charles de Gaulle and Free French leaders were not happy to leave their eight newly formed divisions in Italy and the Mediterranean theater, and were pressuring the US government to commit them to the liberation of France. (NARA)

Heeresgruppe G lost more than half its forces, totaling over 150,000 troops as well as most of its heavy equipment. In the space of less than four weeks, the majority of France was liberated at very modest cost to Allied forces. The main operational objective was to capture the ports of Marseille and Toulon and these would prove essential to the support of the Allied operations, providing more than a quarter of all Allied supplies in 1944–45. *Dragoon* was a textbook example of the Allies' enormous advantage in operational mobility via amphibious operations. It effectively exploited the Wehrmacht's strategic overextension caused by Hitler's stubborn refusal to consolidate to more defensible positions in 1944.

THE STRATEGIC SITUATION

The 1943 Allied decision to invade Normandy in 1944 set the stage for further debates about the use of Allied forces in the Mediterranean theater of operations (MTO). The American viewpoint, most strongly argued by Chief of Staff General George C. Marshall, was that the Mediterranean theater represented a wasteful diversion and that further operations in Italy should be limited except for the need to tie down German forces. British strategy had traditionally favored peripheral operations, and British political interests in the Mediterranean also encouraged more extensive operations there, beyond Italy into Greece and the Balkans.

The American proposal to stage an amphibious landing in southern France was first broached at the Trident conference in May 1943, one of a series of conferences sponsored by the Combined Chiefs of Staff (CCS). Such an operation was too risky to conduct in 1943, and at the time of the Quadrant conference in August 1943 between Roosevelt and Churchill, the US Joint Chiefs of Staff were promoting an amphibious operation in southern France, codenamed *Anvil*, that could be launched around the same time as Operation *Overlord* in Normandy. The British opposed the plan, favoring continued operations in Italy or elsewhere in the Mediterranean. When the issue was raised at a conference with Stalin in Tehran on November 28, 1943, the Soviets were adamant that *Overlord* go ahead in May 1944 as promised, and showed no enthusiasm at all for further operations in the Mediterranean except for *Anvil* which they viewed as an intriguing adjunct to *Overlord*. The conference concluded with the Combined Chiefs of Staff agreeing to limit Italian offensives beyond Rome and instead to focus on a combined *Overlord–Anvil* operation in May 1944. The prospects for *Anvil* dimmed considerably in early 1944. Both Montgomery and Eisenhower agreed that more amphibious landing capability would be need for the Normandy operation, and this absorbed some of the resources planned for *Anvil*. At the same time, Allied operations in Italy had gone badly. The US Army had reluctantly agreed to an amphibious landing at Anzio in January 1944 as a means to speed up the capture of Rome. Starved of troops and supplies, the Anzio operation soon stalled and turned into a bloody battle of attrition. British planners argued that the Allies could not support three major operations—Italy, *Overlord*, and *Anvil*—simultaneously and that *Anvil* should be sacrificed. So *Anvil* went into limbo in the spring of 1944.

The prospects for a southern France operation revived in June 1944 after the capture of Rome and the Normandy landings. The successful conclusion of the Normandy landing freed up amphibious assets and the liberation of

Rome ended the frustrations around Monte Cassino and Anzio. The tipping point was the Channel storm on the Normandy coast in late June that wrecked the artificial harbor on Omaha Beach and the German demolition of the port of Cherbourg prior to its capture by the US Army. Eisenhower became very concerned about port capacity to supply Allied forces, and the seizure of the ports of Marseille and Toulon became increasingly attractive. On the political front, de Gaulle and the Free French leaders were not happy to see the growing French army in the Mediterranean squandered in pointless attritional warfare in the Italian mountains, and demanded that they be employed in France. Churchill realized that *Anvil* would strangle his cherished Italian campaign and he made a last-minute plea to Roosevelt labeling the operation "a major strategic and political error." Based on Marshall's advice, Roosevelt rebuffed Churchill and refused any Balkan adventures. The Combined Chiefs of Staff authorized the southern France landings on July 14, 1944. The revived plan received a new codename, *Dragoon*, reputedly offered by Churchill who complained that he had been "dragooned" into the operation.

While northern France had been occupied by the Wehrmacht since the 1940 armistice, France south of the Loire had remained under Maréchal Pétain's French Government based in Vichy. When the Allies invaded French North Africa in November 1942, the Wehrmacht occupied the remainder of France except for the Riviera coast, which was occupied by the Italian Fourth Army. When Italy signed an armistice with the Allies on September 8, 1943, the Wehrmacht occupied the rest of the Riviera coast. Southern France did not play a major role in German strategic planning and served mainly as a training area for units later dispatched back to Russia or to Italy. With Allied operations against southern France growing more likely in late 1943 and early 1944, local commanders hoped that Berlin would permit a strategic realignment akin to the strategic withdrawal to the Hindenburg Line in 1917. In this case a withdrawal of Heeresgruppe G back toward Dijon would create

The senior Allied commanders discuss Operation *Dragoon*. From left to right, Seventh Army commander Lieutenant-General Alexander Patch; French War Minister André Diethelm; 1ère Armée Française commander Général Jean de Lattre; Supreme Commander Allied Forces Mediterranean General Sir Henry Maitland Wilson; and 12th Army Group commander General Jacob Devers. (NARA)

a more viable defensive perimeter shielding Alsace, Lorraine and the Saar. Given Hitler's penchant for clinging to every last bit of conquered territory, such a realignment was not seriously contemplated until it was too late.

By midsummer 1944, the Allies had four strategic advantages over the Wehrmacht in southern France: mobility, counter-mobility, intelligence and communication. The operational mobility offered by Allied naval dominance made it difficult for the Wehrmacht to concentrate its forces to repel an amphibious invasion since it could strike nearly anywhere from Bordeaux on the Atlantic coast to the Greek islands in the eastern Mediterranean. Allied airpower exacerbated this dilemma since bombers could deny the Wehrmacht the mobility to mass its forces for a counterattack both by bombing key bridges as well as by attacking German forces during movement. The Allies enjoyed substantial intelligence advantages at nearly all levels including photoreconnaissance and local intelligence from the French resistance. Heeresgruppe G's tactical communication within the theater as well as operational links to headquarters in Paris and Berlin were very brittle owing to dependence on the French telephone networks. Once the French resistance severed these, German operational orders had to be forwarded by radio, exposing them to the Ultra codebreakers and amplifying the Allied intelligence advantage.

CHRONOLOGY

1942

November 11,   After Allied landings in French North Africa, Wehrmacht launches Operation *Anton*, occupying Vichy France; Provence occupied by the Italian Fourth Army.

1943

May 12–25   Idea of landings in southern France first raised at Trident conference.

August 17–24   Operation *Anvil* formally proposed at Quadrant conference.

September 8   Italy signs armistice with Allies; Wehrmacht activates Plan *Achse*, disarms Italian Fourth Army on the Riviera, extends occupation to all of Provence.

November 28   Stalin formally supports *Anvil* at Teheran conference.

1944

July 14   *Anvil* revived and formally approved by Combined Chiefs of Staff.

August 1   Southern France operation redesignated as *Dragoon*.

August 4   Mediterranean Tactical Air Force release final *Dragoon* bombing plan, increasing the air campaign over Provence.

August 10   Operation *Nutmeg* begins major bombing campaign against coastal artillery and radar sites in Provence.

August 15   Operation *Dragoon* begins in pre-dawn hours with deception actions along coast; H-Hour is 0800hrs.

August 16	Hitler accepts OKW plan to authorize Heeresgruppe G withdrawal from southern France.
August 17	OKW orders dispatched to Heeresgruppe G in two parts at 0940 and 1730hrs; later part not received until 1100hrs August 18.
August 19	US VI Corps takes Brignoles and Barjols on the approaches to Aix-en-Provence.
August 19	French forces begin to envelope Toulon
August 21	157. Reserve-Division abandons Grenoble, US and French FFI take control on August 22.
August 21	Elements of TF Butler reach Hill 300 overlooking Route 7 north of Montélimar starting the fight for the Montélimar "battle square."
August 25	AOK 19 counterattack on 36th Division defensive line along Roubion River fizzles out.
August 26	With most of Toulon liberated, French army stages victory march in the city.
August 27	Last major German strongholds in Marseille surrender.
August 28	Last German hold-outs of Toulon garrison surrender at dawn on Saint-Mandrier Peninsula.
August 29	Last German rearguards overwhelmed at Montélimar; Heeresgruppe G crossing Drôme River further north.
September 3	Lyon liberated.
September 10–14	Patrols of Patton's Third Army begin encountering patrols from Patch's Seventh Army linking the Normandy and *Dragoon* landings.
September 14	Patch orders VI Corps to halt operations; control of *Dragoon* forces passes from Mediterranean command to Eisenhower's SHAEF command.
September 15	Last march-group from AOK 1 capitulates on Loire River; 20,000 troops surrender.

OPPOSING COMMANDERS

GERMAN COMMANDERS

The Wehrmacht in southern France had a complex and dysfunctional command network. The Heer (army) had a bifurcated command structure with a parallel command network for the military occupation government and the tactical forces. The Kreigsmarine (navy) had a separate command network that was vertically integrated to central naval commands in Paris, not to local army commands. While this would ordinarily have been of little importance in land combat, it was a significant tactical distraction due to the Kriegmarine's major role in coastal defense along the Mediterranean. This fragile network was further weakened in August 1944 when German headquarters began to abandon their offices in Paris. While the Kriegsmarine and Heer did their best to work around these problems, the Luftwaffe command remained aloof and fought their own war. For example, the Luftwaffe proved unwilling to train or deploy their numerous flak units for secondary missions against ground targets or for shore defense.

After the occupation of southern France in November 1942, the Militärbefehlshaber in Frankreich (MBH: Military Governor in France)

Generaloberst Johannes Blaskowitz, commander of Heeresgruppe G. (MHI)

General der Infanterie Friedrich Wiese, commander of AOK 19. (MHI)

Generalmajor Ludwig Bieringer, military governor of the Var department, commanding Verbindgungsstab 800, which directed the Wehrmacht's occupation forces in the region. (NARA)

established the Heersgebiet Südfrankreich (HGSF: Army District Southern France) under Generalleutnant Heinrich Niehoff. Headquartered in Lyon, this command was responsible for occupation duties and controlled most security units in southern France except for the tactical units along the coast.

The army tactical combat units in central, western and southern France were commanded by Heeresgruppe G; its two subordinate commands were Armeeoberkommando 1 (AOK 1: First Army) on the Atlantic coast from Spain to the Loire estuary, and AOK 19 on the French Mediterranean coast. Heeresgruppe G was commanded by General der Infanterie Johannes Blaskowitz. Although from East Prussia, he was not from a traditional military family and his father was a Lutheran minister. He served as a young officer in the infantry in World War I, first on the French front including Verdun, later in Serbia and Russia, and ending the war as a captain with the Iron Cross first and second class. He remained in the Reichswehr after the war, steadily advancing in rank and becoming a *Generalmajor* in October 1932. He was apolitical but strongly nationalistic, so his career continued to advance after the rise of the Nazis. General der Infanterie Günther Blumentritt later recalled that he was "rigorously just and high-minded … with a strong spiritual and religious turn of mind." This would not serve him well with the Nazis. Blaskowitz led AOK 8 during the invasion of Poland, fighting the most intense battle of the campaign during the Polish counterattack on the Bzura River. In the wake of the campaign, he complained about the atrocities against Poles and Jews by the SS. He remained in Poland as Commander-in-Chief East through the spring of 1940 but ran afoul of Hitler's governor-general, Hans Frank, who had him removed in May 1940. Hitler dismissed his complaints about SS brutality as "childish ideas" and Blaskowitz was sidetracked to occupation duty in France, commanding AOK 1 on the Bay of Biscay. Although not favored by the Nazis, he had the support of the Heeresgruppe B commander in northern France, Generalfeldmarschall Gerd von Rundstedt, and in May 1944, Blaskowitz was placed in command of Heeresgruppe G.

The headquarters of AOK 19 was led by General der Infanterie Georg von Sodenstern until June 1944, but he ran afoul of Rommel after vigorously contesting his tactics for coastal defense. General der Infanterie Friedrich Wiese replaced him. Wiese had served in World War I, and in 1919 had been a member of the Freikorps. Unlike Blaskowitz, he was regarded as a fervent Nazi. He led an infantry battalion in Poland in 1939, a regiment in France in 1940 and was promoted to command 26. Infanterie-Division in April 1942 while on the Russian Front. Wiese became commander of 35. Armee Korps (AK) in Heeresgruppe Mitte in August 1943, and was promoted to *General der Infanterie* that October. He had a distinguished career as a Russian Front commander, decorated with the Knight's Cross in February 1942 and the Knight's Cross with Oak leaves in January 1944. He remained in corps command until days before the Soviet Operation *Bagration* offensive in late June 1944 that destroyed the corps; he had been assigned instead to lead AOK 19 in June 1944, arriving in southern France in July.

The element of AOK 19 most directly connected with Operation *Dragoon* was 62. AK commanded by General der Infanterie Ferdinand Neuling. He would play little role in the campaign as his headquarters was located near the Allied paratroop drop zone and he was quickly captured.

German naval forces on the French Mediterranean coast were under the command of Admiral Französische Südküste headquartered in Aix-en-

Provence. Vizeadmiral Paul Wever was in command until August 11 when he died of a heart attack. He was replaced by Ernst Scheurlen who did not arrive until August 17 after the invasion had taken place. Scheurlen was a rare example of a Kriegsmarine officer specializing in coastal artillery and his selection was a recognition that navy dispositions on the French Mediterranean lacked any significant warships and depended largely on coastal artillery.

ALLIED COMMANDERS

The senior command of Operation *Dragoon* varied depending upon the phase of the mission. The Mediterranean theater was under the command of Allied Forces Headquarters (AFHQ) led by General Sir Henry Maitland Wilson of the British Army. Wilson's deputy commander was American Lieutenant-General Jacob Devers and in July 1944, Wilson appointed Devers to the Advanced Detachment AFHQ which served as a link between AFHQ and Seventh Army during the planning of Operation *Dragoon*. Although the US Seventh Army would conduct the initial amphibious landings, the follow-on force was primarily the 1ère Armée Française. The French promoted the idea of a senior French commander over both, but neither the Americans nor British were content with such an arrangement. The 1ère Armée Française had been raised and equipped by the US Army and was still heavily dependent on the US for administrative and logistical support; an army group headquarters would coordinate with Anglo-American higher headquarters and regional commands where the French had no experience. British and American commanders agreed to the formation of the 6th Army Group to manage the US Seventh and 1ère Française armies once all their forces were ashore; at this point, command would shift from Wilson in the Mediterranean theater to Eisenhower in the European theater. Devers became 6th Army Group commander on July 16, 1944, though the actual activation of the headquarters did not take place until mid-September after *Dragoon* had concluded.

Lieutenant-General Alexander Patch, commander US Seventh Army. (NARA)

BELOW
VI Corps commander Major-General Lucian Truscott to the left and Major-General John "Iron Mike" O'Daniel, commander of the 3rd Division to the right. (NARA)

Major-General John E. Dahlquist, commander of the 36th Division. (NARA)

Seventh Army had been headed by George S. Patton during the Sicily operation, but when he transferred to Britain in early 1944, the spot was left vacant. The initial presumption was that the Fifth Army commander, Mark Clark, would take over Operation *Anvil* but this was derailed in February 1944 owing to the ill-fated Anzio landings which demanded his full attention. The newly arrived IV Corps commander, Major-General Alexander Patch, was given the command instead. Patch was born at Fort Huachuca in the Arizona territory as the son of a 4th Cavalry officer and graduated from West Point in 1913. He returned to the southwest to serve in Pershing's expedition in Mexico, and commanded an infantry battalion in France in 1918. In early 1942, Patch was assigned to command a task force headed to Guadalcanal that eventually became the Americal Division. After leading the new division in combat in the Army's first major offensive campaign, Patch commanded XIV Corps on Guadalcanal until the Japanese defenders were finally subdued in early 1943. Patch returned to the United States to train the new IV Corps which was sent to the Mediterranean in early 1944. He was not especially favored by either Marshall or Eisenhower, but he was championed by Eisenhower's chief of staff, General Walter Bedell-Smith and so appointed to Seventh Army command.

The senior US tactical commander during Operation *Dragoon* was Major-General Lucian Truscott who led VI Corps. Truscott had served as a young cavalry officer in World War I and was instrumental in the formation of the 1st Ranger Battalion in 1942. He led a task force under General George S. Patton during the Operation *Torch* landings in French North Africa in November 1942. While serving as a deputy to Eisenhower in Tunisia, he was assigned to command 3rd Infantry Division in April 1943 in the wake of the Kasserine Pass debacle. He led the division during the amphibious landings at Sicily, Salerno and Anzio, and took over corps command at Anzio in February 1944 because of widespread dissatisfaction over the performance of General John Lucas. Truscott was highly regarded by Eisenhower who wanted him for Normandy, but the demands of the Anzio campaign kept him in the Mediterranean.

The senior French army commander for Operation *Dragoon* was Général Jean de Lattre de Tassigny. He graduated from Saint-Cyr in 1911 and first served in the cavalry. After being wounded twice in the opening months of World War I, he transferred to the infantry serving at Verdun and the failed Nivelle Offensive of 1917. After the war he transferred to Morocco and took part in the pacification campaigns there and in the Rif War where he was wounded a fifth time in 1925. He was posted to the General Staff under Général Weygand in 1931; his rival for the post was Charles de Gaulle. He led the 14e Division d'infanterie in the battle of France in 1940 and the division put up a spirited defense near Rethel, remaining a coherent fighting force through its retreat. De Lattre was not captured by the Germans but owing to his loyalty to Weygand, he decided to remain in France rather than join de Gaulle's Free French movement abroad. He served in the Vichy French Armistice Army in metropolitan France and Tunisia, but sided with anti-German factions. De Lattre was arrested and imprisoned by the Vichy Government in November 1942 after the Wehrmacht occupied Vichy France. In September 1943, he broke out of prison and escaped to Britain. De Gaulle recognized his talent and experience and dispatched him to Algeria to help raise the expanding French army there. By early 1944, two major French forces were already formed, an expeditionary force of four divisions under

Senior French and American commanders at the Belfort lion monument from left to right, Général Jean de Lattre de Tassigny, commander of the 1ère Armée Française; Lieutenant-General Jacob Devers, commander of the 6th Army Group, Général M. E. Bethuouard, commander of the French 1er Corps; and Général Joseph de Goislard de Monsabert, commander of the French 3e Division during Operation *Dragoon* but subsequently French IIe Corps commander after de Lattre got rid of rival Général de Larminat. (NARA)

Général Alphonse Juin serving with the Allies in Italy on the Monte Cassino front, and LeClerc's 2e Division blindée, the showcase French formation earmarked for operations in France. De Lattre had to make do with what was left, while at the same time pushing to secure the return of Juin's force to bolster any French army operating in southern France. In April 1944, de Lattre was assigned to command Army B, the force assigned to the proposed Allied landing in southern France. As a preliminary operation, de Lattre commanded the capture of the island of Elba on June 17, 1944, by a combined force of the Royal Navy, the new 9e DIC (Division d'infanterie coloniale) and French special forces.

The commander of the French II Corps d'armée was Général Edgard de Larminat. However, de Larminat and de Lattre had major disagreements about tactics for the Provence campaign and following the landings, de Lattre took over active command of the corps and pushed aside de Larminat.

Allied naval units in the Mediterranean were led by Commander-in-Chief, Mediterranean Admiral Sir John H. D. Cunningham. To manage the naval aspects of Operation *Dragoon*, he created the Western Naval Task Force under the US Eighth Fleet commander, Vice Admiral Henry Hewitt. The air commander in the theater was Lieutenant-General Ira Eaker who served both as Commander-in-Chief Mediterranean Allied Air Forces (MAAF) but also as the commander of the US Army Air Forces under NATOUSA.

OPPOSING FORCES

WEHRMACHT

Heeresgruppe G and AOK 19 saw a steady degradation of their combat power in 1944 prior to Operation *Dragoon*. Units were siphoned off in January–February 1944 to reinforce counterattacks against the Anzio beachhead in Italy. Strength had rebounded by the early summer, only to see extensive new diversions to Normandy starting in June. Aside from the sheer numbers of troops sent to Normandy, the best quality units were stripped away. For example, most of the Panzer corps in southern France in June 1944, including the 2. SS-Panzer-Division, 9. Panzer-Division, and 17. SS-Panzergrenadier-Division were all sent to Normandy, leaving only the 11. Panzer-Division and even that division lost one of its two tank battalions.

Of the 13 infantry divisions in Heeresgruppe B in June 1944, only four were so-called "assault" divisions, meaning full-strength infantry divisions under the new 1944 tables that were capable of offensive action; all but one were sent to Normandy. The remaining nine divisions consisted of four static and five reserve divisions. The static (*bodenständig*) divisions were primarily intended to man coastal defenses and were stretched very thinly along the Mediterranean an average of 56 miles per division, more than five times

The only major element of AOK 19 not stationed on the Mediterranean coast was 157. Reserve-Division, located in the mountains of the Alpes-Maritimes near Grenoble to combat the French FFI. This is a patrol from Res.Pz.Jag.Kp. 7 based in Chambéry with an Italian AB-41 armored car on the left and an SdKfz 7/1 half-track armed with a quad 20mm Flak 38 behind. (NARA)

the recommended defensive frontage. In general, the troops in these divisions were second or third rate, consisting of older veterans, wounded soldiers not fit for more active assignments and *Volksdeutsche* recruited from regions of Poland and the Czech lands incorporated into the Reich. Through much of 1943 and early 1944, these units were further weakened by "combing" their battalions of the fittest soldiers to help rebuild other infantry formations destined for Russia. A number of units were also subjected to "dilution" by transfer of battalions to Russia while substituting *Ost* (East) battalions made up of Soviet prisoners of war who had volunteered to serve in the Wehrmacht rather than starve to death in the prison camps. The static divisions were generally armed with captured weapons or weapons considered obsolete on the combat fronts and they had little transport. To make up for their manpower weaknesses, the static divisions were usually deployed in field fortifications and issued a larger number of support weapons.

The five reserve divisions were nominally intended to serve as training formations, but in reality they were more often used for construction work on the defensive bunkers being created along the coast, as well as for security and anti-partisan actions. In general, these units had better manpower than the static divisions, though not comparable to full-strength "assault" divisions. The one exception was the 157. Reserve-Division; it was the only AOK 19 division stationed away from the coast near Grenoble to fight against the growing activity of French resistance units and it was kept at fighting strength.

The unit directly in the path of Operation *Dragoon* was 242. Infanterie-Division headquartered in Hyères. This static division was assigned about 90 miles of coastline from Cap Dramont near Saint-Raphaël in the east to Cap Sicié west of Toulon. The division had been formed in July 1943 mostly from depot troops and dispatched to Belgium for occupation and training duties. By July 1944, it was near full strength with 12,000 troops, but three of its 12 infantry battalions were replaced with Armenian and Azerbaijani *Ost* battalions in April 1944. The division's equipment was a hodgepodge of leftovers, with French and Italian weapons predominating; many of the Soviet, Czech and Polish weapons listed below came secondhand from the Italians. Instead of the standard German MG34/42, the division's machine guns included at least 13 types including Italian 6.5mm, 8mm and 13.2mm machine guns, Polish 7.62mm Maxims and Brownings, three different French machines in different calibers, and a mixture of German machine guns including World War I Maxims and some MG34s. To make up for its excessive frontage, the division had an unusually large amount of small-caliber artillery beyond the usual divisional tables. For example, besides its usual 75mm PaK 40 anti-tank guns, it had 36 additional obsolete anti-tank guns for coastal defense, which included French 25mm and 47mm, German 37mm and 75mm, Soviet 45mm, Czech 47mm and Italian 47mm guns. It also had several dozen assorted World War I French and Italian light field guns also used for coastal defense. The division's infantry mortars were mostly Italian 45mm and 81mm and French 81mm types. While this might seem to be a logistical nightmare, in fact the division was limited to whatever ammunition was on hand as it lacked the transport for re-supply once the fighting began. So the divisions generally received a higher allotment of artillery and mortar ammunition than usual, on average six units of fire, compared with only two units of fire issued to units in Normandy. (A unit of fire is an amount of ammunition roughly equivalent to an average day's usage in combat; a unit of fire for a light field howitzer battery was 900 rounds.)

The division's artillery regiment had three field artillery battalions each equipped with different guns: the Yugoslav Skoda M28 100mm field howitzers (FH317j), Italian Skoda 100/17 field howitzers (FH315i), and Czech Skoda M14/19 100mm field howitzers (FH14/19t). As is mentioned in more detail below, the divisions were supported by an extensive array of coastal artillery units so that in 242. Infanterie-Division's sector, there were 106 additional artillery pieces beyond the division's own field guns. As befit its name, the division was almost completely static and over the course of 1944 its horses and carts were gradually stripped away. Only one company in each battalion was nominally equipped with bicycles to serve as a mobile force.

The neighboring divisions presented much the same picture. The other division of the 62. AK was 148. Reserve-Infanterie-Division to the east of 242. Infanterie-Division, which covered the Riviera coast up to the Italian border. It was near full strength, but thinly stretched along 60 miles of coast. Besides its 36 divisional guns, there were a further 28 guns for coastal defense in its sector. One of its *Ost* battalions was located on the eastern fringe of the *Dragoon* beaches. To the west of 242. Infanterie-Division was the 85. AK's 244. Infanterie-Division, another static division covering 80km of coastline in Marseille and the Bouches-du-Rhône department. This division would be central in the battle for Marseille. It had 11,640 troops in the summer of 1944 including 440 Russian and Italian auxiliaries. Coastal defense batteries added a further 86 guns in this sector.

Heeresgruppe G's principal reserve was 11. Panzer-Division, the only significant mechanized unit remaining in southern and central France. It had been moved to the Toulouse area so that it could intervene either westward in the AOK 1 sector around Bordeaux should the Allies land on the Bay of Biscay, or eastward toward Marseille or Toulon if the Allies landed there. The division had recently been re-built in the Bordeaux area starting in May after having been smashed during the encirclement at Kamenets-Podolsk in the spring of 1944. By August it was approaching full strength, even if training was incomplete owing to growing fuel shortages. In the weeks before *Dragoon*, half of its tank strength was sent to Normandy. The survival of much of Heeresgruppe G would depend on its combat performance.

Behind the thin crust of coastal defenses, the interior was patrolled by the security units of Heeresgebiet Südfrankreich (HGS) organized into several Verbindungsstäbe (liaison staffs) which corresponded with French administrative departments. So for example, the Var department, where the *Dragoon* landings would take place, was the responsibility of Verbindgungsstab 800, commanded by Generalmajor Ludwig Bieringer. The Wehrmacht occupation effort ran in parallel to a substantial German police presence in southern France including the field elements of the Gestapo such as the Sipo (Sicherheitspolizei), and SD (Sicherheitsdienst).

The security units were involved in continual actions against the French resistance through 1944, and there was a major upsurge in violence on both sides in the summer of 1944 as the guerilla war escalated. A French officer who clandestinely visited Provence in July 1944 reported back that:

> No isolated German car, no courier could travel the highways, no enemy roadblocks, no control existed outside the garrison towns. No traces of military works or mine fields. The Germans are practically prisoners in their

garrisons, from which they only emerge in force for supplies or on a reprisal expedition—and half the time these convoys are attacked by an uncatchable enemy. After a couple months of this situation, the German soldier is bewildered, demoralized, fooled—we know this, we steal his mail. He looks with fear on these mountains, these forests, these crags, these narrow valleys from which any moment, a thunderbolt can crash. He awaits the arrival of the "regulars," the Allied soldiers, for deliverance.

WEHRMACHT ORDER OF BATTLE, PROVENCE COAST, AUGUST 1944

Armeeoberkommando. 19 (AOK 19)	Avignon	Gen. Friedrich Wiese
Arko 219	Draguignan	Obst. Wolfgang Neuling
Festung-Pionier-Kommandeur. 1	Remoulins	Gen.Maj. René Eberle
62. Armee Korps	Draguignan	Gen. Ferdinand Neuling
Festung-Pionier-Stab 14	Petits Esclans	
242. Infanterie-Division (*bodenständig*)	Hyères	Gen.Lt. Johannes Baeßler
GR 917	Bormes-les-Mimosas	
GR 918	Valette-Baudouvin	
GR 765	Le Muy	
AR 242	La Farède	
148. Reserve-Infanterie Division	Grasse	Gen.Maj. Otto Fretter Pico
Res.GR 8	Nice Saint-Pons	
Res.GR 239	Vallauris	
Res.AR 8	Grasse	
85. Armee Korps	Marseille	Gen. der Inf. Baptist Kneiss
Festung-Pionier-Stab 3	Luynes	
244. Infanterie-Division (*bodenständig*)	Aubagne	Gen.Lt. Hans Schaefer
GR 932	Marseille–Saint-Antoine	
GR 933	Aubagne	
GR 934	Col de l'Agne	
AR 244	Saint-Marcel	
338. Infanterie-Division (*bodenständig*)	Chateau de Berbegal (Arles)	Gen.Lt. René l'Homme de Courbière
GR 757	Montpellier	
GR 758	Martigues	
GR 759	Chateau d'Avignon	
AR 338	Arles	
Heersgebiet Südfrankreich	Lyon	Gen.Lt. Heinrich Niehoff
Oberfeldkommandantur 894	Marseille	Gen.Maj. Rudolf Hünermann
VS 747	Gard/Nîmes	
VS 761	Vaucluse/Avignon	
VS 497	Bouches-du-Rhône /Marseille	
VS 800	Var/Draguignan	
VS 994	Alpes-Maritimes/Nice	
VS 792	Basses-Alpes/Digne	
VS 555	Hautes-Alpes/Gap	

GR: Grenadier Regiment; AR: Artillerie Regiment; VS: Verbindungsstab

Südwall

In 1943, the Wehrmacht began extending the Atlantikwall coastal fortifications to the Mediterranean coast, sometimes dubbed the Südwall (South Wall). The French Mediterranean coast had been fortified since ancient times, and there had been a major fortification effort under Vauban in the 1680s, modernized continuously ever since. The old strongholds played a significant role in the 1944 campaign, especially in the fighting for Toulon and Marseille. The French Navy modernized some of the major coastal defenses in the 1930s, especially around the major ports. Following the French defeat in 1940, the Italian Army occupied the Riviera, including the Var department, as far as Toulon. The Italians added many small fortifications and gun positions along the coast but the Italian construction was mostly small pillboxes made of ordinary concrete without steel reinforcement, which were not especially durable against naval gunfire. Following the September 1943 armistice, the Wehrmacht absorbed the 120 Italian artillery batteries along the coast and these formed the initial core of German coastal defenses along the Var coast. There were friendly relations between some Wehrmacht and Italian units, and a significant number of Italian troops decided to remain under Wehrmacht command rather than end up in prisoner-of-war camps. Some German coastal artillery batteries were filled out by as much as a third with Italian auxiliaries.

Organization Todt (OT), the paramilitary construction agency, began the Südwall fortification program in early 1943 along the western portions of the Provence coast. Since the Var coast did not come under German control until after the September 1943 armistice, its fortifications were especially thin. After Allied bombing raids had knocked out a number of coastal batteries on the Atlantic coast, during Christmas 1943 Hitler ordered an emergency gun fortification program and OT was assigned to fortify 400 guns on the Mediterranean coast by April 1944. As a result, about 78 percent of the gun bunkers were completed, but less than half of the other bunkers. Hitler's gun casemate program was a mixed blessing; even though it offered better protection from air attack it limited the gun traverse to 120 degrees seaward and so the batteries were useless during the ensuing port battles since they could not fire against land targets. The coastal defense efforts were concentrated near ports such as Toulon and Marseille, while much of the Var coast in between had few fortified positions. Toulon had 24 strongpoints, manned by 1,590 troops and armed with 141 machine guns, 11 mortars, 23 Flak guns, and 22 field guns.

One of the most common defenses on the Var coast was the Panzerturm consisting of the turret from an obsolete tank such as this PzKpfw II mounted on a concrete foundation. (NARA)

ORGANIZATION TODT FORTIFICATION: MEDITERRANEAN COAST 1944

Type	Planned	Completed
Ammunition bunker	337	150
Command bunker	28	14
Observation bunker	34	16
Hospital bunker	22	18
Communication bunker	10	2
Gun casemate	482	381
Open gun platform	47	30
Field fortification	584	281
Total	1,544	892

The Batterie Mauvannes was supported by this camouflaged M262a two-story fire-control bunker. These bunkers contained rangefinders to locate and track enemy warships, plotting tables to prepare firing data, and communication equipment to pass the information to the gun batteries. (NARA)

In place of formal steel-reinforced concrete bunkers, many of the infantry divisions and coastal batteries were obliged to make do with improvised defenses using local construction such as log-reinforced gun pits. One speedy method to create fortified defenses was to mount tank turrets from obsolete German tanks or captured French tanks on concrete bases. These were widely used around the Mediterranean ports and by the beginning of 1944 in the AOK 19 sector there were 222 of these including 117 PzKpfw II, 57 PzKpfw 38(t), 28 Somua S-35 and 20 French APX-R 37mm turrets.

The Mediterranean coastline was erratically protected by shore obstacles which were constructed under the direction of the three corps-level engineer regiments, Fest.Pi.Stab 24, 3 and 14 (Festung-Pionier-Stab). Of the 193 miles of coast that were supposed to be defended by obstacles, only 54 miles were completed. It is worth noting that the Var/Riviera coastline where the *Dragoon* landings took place had the weakest coastal obstruction belts. Mines were not widely deployed on the beaches but there were significant minefields further inland with some 1,502,000 in place by August 1944.

Fest.Pi.Stab Sector	24	3	14	Total
Corps	4. LFK	85. AK	62. AK	
Planned length (km)	53	86	52	191
Completed	12	18	23	53
In construction (7/44)	9	12	0	21
Concrete stake	0	70	0	70
Wooden stakes	6,973	7,077	6,748	20,798
Mines	217	831	710	1,758
Concrete tetrahedrons	1,614	3,251	2,793	7,658
Other	40	231	0	271
Obstacles per mile	737	637	446	577

Owing to the meager deployments of infantry, coastal artillery played an unusually prominent role in the defense of the Mediterranean coast, accounting for about a third of the combat troops, and about half of the artillery deployed by AOK 1 and AOK 19. However, the density was not especially great, an average of less than one gun per mile of coastline in AOK 19's 400-mile sector. Furthermore, average density is misleading since the artillery tended to be very dense around the ports and very sparse between the ports.

The army coastal artillery in the 62. AK sector included 11 Heeres-Artillerie-Abteilungen (HAA: army coastal artillery battalion) each with three batteries of four guns each, for a total of 132 guns. The weapons were the usual assortment of captured Italian and French guns, with the Italian 149mm 149/11 (FH404) field howitzer being the most common type equipping seven of the battalions. The Kriesgsmarine coastal artillery regiments were concentrated most heavily around major ports such as Toulon and Marseille; in total there were five normal battalions and one light battalion on the Mediterranean coast. The heaviest concentration of the naval coastal batteries in the 242. Infanterie-Division sector was Toulon where the eight batteries of leicht-Marine-Artillerie-Abteilung 682 (leMAA: light navy artillery battalion) were stationed.

The Wehrmacht did not have the time or resources to fortify the Mediterranean coast as extensively as Normandy and many gun positions were improvised. This is a captured French 75mm mle. 36 anti-aircraft gun set up for beach defense on Cavalaire Bay/Beach Alpha Red.

One of the most formidable defenses on the approach to Toulon was the Batterie Mauvannes of 3./MAA 627 which was overwhelmed in a "mad assault" by the commandos d'Afrique on August 18 with about 50 of its gun crew killed and 100 captured. The battery consisted of four turreted 150mm TbKC/36 naval guns in M272 casemates. (NARA)

Aside from its important role in coastal defense, the Kriegsmarine on the French Mediterranean coast had been largely defanged by the time of the *Dragoon* landings. Its most significant tactical element, 7. U-Boot-Flotilla based in Toulon, had been rendered ineffective by a vigorous Allied anti-submarine warfare campaign in the spring and early summer of 1944 that sank five of its 15 U-boats. Lacking the heavy bunkers found on the Atlantic coast, the submarine docks were subjected to two punishing air raids on Toulon on July 5 and August 6, 1944, which sank the remaining U-boats but for a single one. The 6. Sicherungs-Flotilla based in Marseille was primarily oriented toward the convoy-escort mission and posed little threat to the Allied amphibious operations. It was equipped mainly with small coastal warships including two ex-French torpedo boats, 32 anti-submarine corvettes, 29 minesweepers, 29 artillery barges, 70 armed fishing trawlers and miscellaneous small craft.

As in the case of the Kriegsmarine, the Luftwaffe in southern France had endured a nearly fatal pounding in 1944, suffering relentless attrition while attempting to take part in air campaigns against the Allied landings at Anzio and in Normandy. The primary offensive units of 2. Fliegerdivision were the torpedo-bombers of KG 26, with the three squadrons operating from La Jasse, Montélimar and Nîmes with a strength on July 31, 1944, of 59 Ju-88A-17 of which only 39 were operational; III./KG 100 had 14 Do-217 armed with anti-ship missiles near Toulouse. Fighter strength in the area was meager with 10 Bf-109G operational with 2./JG 200 in Avignon. One of the most effective roles played by the Luftwaffe in early August was the conduct of reconnaissance missions over Allied ports in Italy, Corsica and Algeria, which provided timely information about the massing of the Allied invasion force. The 2. Fliegerdivision included Flak Brigade 5 which was scattered around southern France in small battery positions mainly to defend airfields.

THE ALLIES

The Western Naval Task Force assigned to *Dragoon* was primarily American but with a substantial British element including a battleship, seven light cruisers, and 24 destroyers; most of the Free French Navy also took part. Prior to *Dragoon*, the US Eighth Fleet in the Mediterranean was limited to a pair of light cruisers, so five battleships and three heavy cruisers were transferred from the Atlantic along with a number of destroyers for *Dragoon*. An aircraft carrier force was also assigned to the mission consisting of seven British and two American escort carriers plus an escort of four air defense cruisers and 13 destroyers. In total, the landing force would include some 843 ships and 1,267 landing craft. The Western Naval Task Force was organized into six task forces: TF80 Control Force based around the command ship USS *Catocin;* TF84, 85 and 86 assigned to each of the three landing beaches; TF86 assigned to the special forces operations; and the carrier force TF88.

Allied air power was likewise dominant in the region. As was the case in Northwest Europe, the destruction of the Luftwaffe was one of the primary objectives of the spring 1944 missions. In August 1944, the Mediterranean Allied Air Force (MAAF) had a variety of resources to support *Dragoon*, though at the same time, it had substantial existing commitments that limited the amount of air power that would be available. The heavy bombers of the 15th Air Force based in Italy were committed to the US Strategic Air Force's bombing campaign against Germany and were available to support *Dragoon* on a very limited basis. The Mediterranean Allied Tactical Air Force (MATAF) was heavily committed to supporting existing operations in Italy, as well as bombing operations in southeastern Europe. To consolidate air support for *Dragoon*, XII Tactical Air Command (TAC) was assigned the primary responsibility. US Navy and Royal Navy carrier-borne fighters totaling some 216 Spitfires, Wildcats and Hellcats, were placed under XII TAC command. The liberation of Corsica in 1943 gave the Allies an array of airfields within tactical range of Provence. By August 1944, Corsica was home to the XII TAC's 12 B-25 and four A-20 bomber squadrons, 15 US P-47 and six P-38 fighter squadrons, 11 British Spitfire squadrons, one Beaufighter night-fighter squadron, four French P-47 and Spitfire squadrons and three photoreconnaissance squadrons totaling some 14 airfields and 2,100 combat aircraft.

US Army

By the summer of 1944, the Anglo-American forces in the Mediterranean were highly experienced in amphibious warfare having participated in large-scale landings in French North Africa in November 1942, Sicily in July 1943, Salerno in September 1943 and Anzio in January 1944. The divisions assigned to Operation *Dragoon* were a bit old and threadbare in their equipment compared with the new divisions in the European Theater of Operations (ETO), but they more than made up for this in combat experience.

The 3rd Infantry Division had taken part in the North Africa landings, the Sicily landings, and the Salerno landings. After a long and arduous campaign in the autumn of 1943, it was pulled out and sent to Anzio, playing a central role in the fighting there until being assigned to garrison Rome as Fifth Army reserve after the capture of the city in June 1944. The 36th Division was raised from the Texas National Guard and first saw combat at Salerno in September 1943. The 36th was dubbed a "hard-luck" division after taking heavy losses in the fighting along the Rapido River in January 1944. It was pulled out of the line in March 1944 for rehabilitation and sent to Anzio in May 1944 for the final push on Rome where it performed extremely well. The 45th Division was raised from National Guard units from the American southwest. It had arrived in the Mediterranean theater in June 1943 and took

part in the Sicily campaign, the Salerno landings, the campaign along the Volturno, and the Anzio landings in January 1944. After taking part in the advance on Rome, it was pulled out of the line in June 1944 for rehabilitation prior to Operation *Dragoon*.

The *Dragoon* plan incorporated an airborne landing to secure the high ground beyond the beachheads. Without an airborne division in the Mediterranean theater, the Seventh Army was forced to create one from the units available, first called the Seventh Army Airborne Division (Provisional), and later the 1st Airborne Task Force (FABTF). It was led by Brigadier-General Robert Frederick who had previously led the "Devil's Brigade," the joint American-Canadian 1st Special Services Force in Italy. The FABTF contained the only large British army element in Operation *Dragoon*, the three battalions of the 2nd Independent Parachute Brigade. Since airborne units were in short supply, a number of non-airborne units were inducted for glider delivery. For example, anti-tank defense was provided by the AT Company of the Japanese-American 442nd Infantry Regiment.

Another improvised formation created for Operation *Dragoon* was its mechanized formation, Task Force Butler. VI Corps had been planning on the use of Combat Command 1 (CC Sudré) of the French 1ère Division blindée as its mobile force, but political and tactical considerations led to abandonment of this plan. However, reports from the French officers who clandestinely visited Provence in July convinced General Truscott of the need for a mobile exploitation force in the event that German resistance collapsed. He appointed the assistant corps commander, Brigadier-General Fred Butler to lead the task force which was based around the 117th Cavalry Reconnaissance Squadron Mechanized (CRSM), tank and tank destroyer companies, and truck-transported infantry.

VI CORPS	MAJ. GEN. LUCIAN TRUSCOTT
3rd Infantry Division	**Maj. Gen. John O'Daniel**
7th Infantry Regiment	
15th Infantry Regiment	
30th Infantry Regiment	
Division artillery (9th, 10th, 39th, 41st FAB*)	
756th Tank Battalion (attached)	
601st Tank Destroyer Battalion (attached)	
36th Division	Maj. Gen. John Dahlquist
141st Infantry Regiment	
142nd Infantry Regiment	
143rd Infantry Regiment	
Division artillery (131st, 132nd, 133rd, 155th FAB)	
753rd Tank Battalion (attached)	
636th Tank Destroyer Battalion (attached)	
45th Division	Maj. Gen. William Eagles
157th Infantry Regiment	
179th Infantry Regiment	
180th Infantry Regiment	
Division artillery (158th, 160th, 171st, 189th FAB)	
191st Tank Battalion (attached)	
645th Tank Destroyer Battalion (attached)	
1st Airborne Task Force	Brig. Gen. Robert Frederick
517th Parachute Regimental Combat Team	
2nd (British) Parachute Brigade	
509th Parachute Battalion	
1/551st Parachute Regiment	
Task Force Butler	Brig. Gen. Fred Butler
117th Reconnaissance Squadron	
2/143rd Infantry Regiment	
59th Armored Field Artillery Battalion	
753rd Tank Battalion (-)	
Co. C, 636th Tank Destroyer Battalion	
Co. F, 344th Engineers	

*FAB = field artillery battalion

French Army

The Operation *Dragoon* plan anticipated that the initial amphibious assault would be undertaken by the US Seventh Army, but that a follow-on force of Free French divisions would arrive over the following month. The history of the Free French forces is too complicated to detail here, but, by the end of 1943,

a total of eight divisions were being raised. The first two, the 2e Division blindée (BD: armored division) and 1ère Division motorisée d'infanterie (1ère DMI), had been aligned with de Gaulle's Free French movement from the outset. The other French divisions were raised from the Armée d'Afrique after the US invasion of French North Africa in November 1942. Four infantry divisions were committed to Italy under Gén. Alphonse Juin with the Corps expéditionnaire Français (CEF) and fought with distinction in the tough mountain fighting near Monte Cassino in early 1944. In the meantime, Gén. Jean de Lattre de Tassigny raised three more divisions, the 1ère and 5e DB and the 9e DIC under Armée B. De Gaulle and the provisional French Government wanted all French units committed to the liberation of France, and so planned to extract the CEF from Italy and amalgamate them with de Lattre's forces. At this point, Armée B would become the 1ère Armée Française. In the event, four French divisions arrived in time to take part in actions in Provence, three infantry divisions (1ère, 3e, 9e) and one armored division (1ère). Besides the divisions, there were a significant number of French Special Forces units that took part in the initial phases of Operation *Dragoon*.

The FFI attempted to liberate the Vercors Plateau in July 1944 but were attacked by the 157. Reserve-Division. To overcome the center of resistance around Vassieux, Luftlandgeschwader 1 landed two companies of Russian/Ukrainian troops of Fallschirm-Battalion "Jungwirth" of the Brandenburg Lehr Battalion by DFS.230 and Go.242 gliders on July 23. The skeletal remains of the gliders were still evident in the fields around Vassieux when Allied forces liberated the area in late August 1944. (NARA)

With the exception of the 1ère DMI, which was equipped by the British, the Free French units raised in North Africa in 1943–44 were armed and equipped by the US Army and followed US organizational patterns. At the same time they retained their French regimental lineage that can lead to some confusion as the infantry divisions bore the traditional French designations of mountain division, colonial division and so on while in fact they had the same organization. Tank units retained their regimental designations though in fact they followed US tank battalion organization. The new divisions were formed from a mixture of sources, in some cases absorbing units from the Armée d'Afrique, and in other cases being formed through conscription in the African colonies. French conscription policy recognized two categories, "Européens" and "Indigènes" referring to French settlers in North Africa and the indigenous Algerian, Tunisian and Moroccan population. Sub-Saharan colonial troops were usually designated as "Sénégalais" though in fact they came from a variety of French colonies including Madagascar, the Ivory Coast and Senegal. The mobilization brought in more "Indigènes" than French, amounting to 105,700 by the end of 1944 compared with 48,400 French settlers. Although the large manpower pool in the colonies provided a welcome source of troops, it had its consequences. The US Army had hoped that the new Free French forces would be largely self-sufficient, but the heavy dependence on illiterate African troops made it difficult to fill all the technical and support positions needed in a modern army. The shortage of literate draftees forced the army to accept French women into the AFAT (Auxiliaire fémenin de l'armée de terre), and they served primarily in technical support roles such as radio operators, typists, drivers and nurses. Of the 250,000 troops eventually deployed with the French First Army, about 5,000 were women. De Gaulle's provisional government wanted as large a fighting army as possible for political reasons, so the US Army was obliged to provide a significant amount of support units.

Two of the French divisions taking part in the Provence campaign, the 1ère DMI and 3e DIA, had seen extensive combat in Italy and were well regarded by the US Army for their combat performance in the tough mountain campaigns. On the other hand, the North African troops were not at all popular amongst the Italians who accused them of raping and pillaging, with the Moroccan troops having an especially tough reputation.

ARMÉE B GÉN. JEAN DE LATTRE DE TASSIGNY

II Corps d'Armée	Gén. Edgard de Larminat
1ère DB (Division blindée)	Gén. de div. Jean Touzet du Vigier
2e RC (Régiment cuirassiers)	
2e RCA (Régiment de chasseurs d'Afrique)	
5e RCA	
1er BZ (Bataillon de zouaves)	
68e RAA (Régiment d'artillerie d'Afrique)	
1ère DMI (Division de marche d'infanterie)	Gén. de div. Diego Brosset
1ère Brigade d'infanterie	
2e Brigade d'infanterie	
4e Brigade d'infanterie	
1er RA (Régiment d'artillerie)	
(combat attachments)	
1er RFM (Régiment de fusiliers-marins)	
8e RCA	
3e DIA (Division d'infanterie Algeriénne)	Gén. de div. Joseph de Goislard de Monsabert
3e RTA (Régiment de tirailleurs Algériens)	
7e RTA	
4e RTT	
67e RAA (Régiment d'artillerie d'Afrique)	
(combat attachments)	
3e RSAR (Régiment de spahis algériens de reconnaissance)	
Battalion du Choc	
9e DIC (Division d'Infanterie Coloniale)	Gén. de div. Magnan
4e RTS (Régiment de tirailleurs sénégalais)	
6e RTS	
13e RTS	
RACM (Régiment d'artillerie colonial du Maroc)	
(combat attachments)	
RICM (Régiment d'infanterie colonial du Maroc)	
RCCC (Régiment colonial de chasseurs de chars)	
Groupe de commandos d'Afrique	

French resistance

French resistance units played a far more active combat role in southern France than in Normandy owing to both the terrain and the circumstances. In the south, the resistance units were called Maquis, from the Corsican word for "bush;" an individual fighter was a maquisard. De Gaulle preferred to call them the FFI (Forces Françaises de l'Interior) as if to suggest they were a unified military force rather than a rambunctious assortment of guerillas. The profusion of resistance units in Provence stemmed in part from the belated German occupation of Vichy France in November 1942. Until that point, the Germans had allowed a French armistice army to exist in unoccupied Vichy France. This was dissolved in November 1942 when the Germans took control of central and southern France, but a significant number of officers and men from these units would form the core of later resistance cells. The growth of the resistance accelerated in 1943 with the German imposition of the STO (*Service du Travail Obligatoire*: forced labor service) and many young French took their chances with the resistance rather than slave labor in Germany. The terrain of southern France fostered the resistance movement since the mountainous

terrain and extensive woods provided natural shelter. The resistance did not prosper in the ports or along the coastline owing to vigorous Gestapo actions that decimated resistance units on many occasions. German occupation forces in the hinterland were thinly spread and not as effective as on the coast.

As in northern France, the resistance sprang up in a spontaneous fashion, often as the military arm of various political parties such as the leftist *Libération*, the communist FTP (Francs-tireurs et partisans), and the Gaullist AS (Armée Secrète). The ORA (Organisation de résistance de l'armée) was based around former members of the armistice army. Toward the end of 1943, most of the groups aligned themselves as the MUR (Mouvements unis de la résistance) except for the FTP. In practice, it was impossible to impose centralized control over the Maquis since by their very nature the groups had to be highly secretive to prevent penetration and destruction by the German Gestapo and their French henchmen, the Milice. By the spring of 1944, the resistance units in Provence numbered about 2,130 armed and 7,595 unarmed MUR activists and 1,580 armed and 2,270 unarmed members of FTP. By way of comparison, the German police had more than 12,000 men in the region. Allied support for the Maquis in southern France was not especially generous owing to indecision over Operation *Anvil*. In 1943–45, the Allies dropped 2.8 tons of arms to the Maquis compared with the delivery of 4.2 tons in Greece, 5.9 tons in Italy and 16.4 tons in Yugoslavia. During 1944, the Maquis in Provence received deliveries of 5,574 Sten guns, 4,415 rifles, 289 machine guns, 22 mortars, 29 PIAT anti-tank launchers as well as a substantial amount of explosives besides the existing inventory of French and captured German weapons.

Allied special operations in southern France were pioneered by the British SOE (Special Operations Executive) and later joined by the American OSS (Office of Strategic Services). In May 1944, the joint Special Project Operations Center (SPOC) was opened in Algiers to coordinate Allied special operations in southern France. The British, French, and Americans all sent their own teams into Provence, as well as inter-Allied teams. There were three specialized types of teams. The Jedburghs were inter-Allied teams, usually of three men, assigned specific missions. Operational Groups were relatively large OSS paratrooper

teams organized into squads of about 30 troops assigned specific combat missions. Counter-scorch teams were a French effort composed of naval personnel who were dispatched to ports such as Toulon and Marseille with the mission to minimize German sabotage of the docks and harbors. Allied special operations intensified as Operation *Dragoon* approached and there were 1,129 sorties into southern France in 1944. The US Seventh Army organized the 4-SFU (Special Forces Unit No. 4) with experienced British and American agents to handle coordination with the Maquis once operations began.

The Normandy landings on June 6, 1944, prompted the Maquis on the remote Vercors Plateau near Grenoble to launch an insurrection, eventually involving some 4,000 fighters. The Wehrmacht counterattacked with 157. Reserve-Division and overwhelmed the Maquis in late July. The bloody suppression of the Vercors insurrection further inflamed the Maquis in the region but also served as a warning that they were not well enough armed or organized to directly confront the Wehrmacht until the arrival of the Allies. They returned to the more traditional style of *petit guerre* (little war) preferring harassment and ambush of German units rather than large-scale tactical operations.

The Maquis played a far more significant military role in the southern France campaign than did their counterparts in Normandy. This machine-gun team is in action in the town of Apt north of Avignon on August 22. (NARA)

OPPOSING PLANS

GERMAN PLANS

Anglo-American naval supremacy in 1944 put great strain on Wehrmacht planning. The Allies could land nearly anywhere on the Greek coast, the Adriatic, southern France or the Bay of Biscay. During the early summer of 1944, four possible landing areas seemed most likely. The southern coast of Brittany near the Loire estuary provided both ports and access to the Loire Valley. The lower Bay of Biscay would provide the prize port of Bordeaux. A landing in southern France would provide ports at Marseille and Toulon, while at the same time offering access to the Rhône Valley. A landing in the Bay of Genoa could follow the Allied pattern of leapfrogging up the western Italian coast with the possibility of cutting off the Wehrmacht in Italy, and driving toward the Brenner Pass and into southeastern Germany. After the Normandy landings in June 1944, OKW assessed the probability of the next Allied landing in the Mediterranean to be the Gulf of Genoa (50 percent), southern France (40 percent) and the Adriatic (10 percent). Corsica was becoming a major hub of Allied air and naval activity and it was equidistant from Genoa and the Provence coast.

For Heeresgruppe G, the most worrying development of midsummer was the advance of Patton's Third Army down the Loire Valley following the Operation *Cobra* breakout in Normandy on July 25, 1944. Patton was racing toward the Dijon area, where he might cut off Heeresgruppe G's supply line to Germany. In desperation, Berlin ordered AOK 1 headquartered in Bordeaux to establish a defensive perimeter in the Loire Valley. Without adequate forces, this was a hopeless task and Third Army overran the meager forces that AOK 1 was able to place in its path such as at Chartres.

Blaskowitz's Heeresgruppe G headquarters opened discussion with Berlin in early August 1944 about withdrawing its forces out of southern France and establishing a new defensive line around Dijon, linked to AOK 1's attempts in the approaches to Paris. The plan was to pull back all of Heeresgruppe G to the Dijon area by August 20, abandoning southern and western France. Since the attempted coup against Hitler on July 20, 1944, recommendations from units in France were viewed with undisguised contempt in Berlin due to the complicity in the coup attempt by several senior commanders in Paris. Although a withdrawal from southern France made good strategic sense, in the paranoid atmosphere in Berlin, it was out of the question.

While Berlin would not countenance a strategic withdrawal of Heeresgruppe G, there were few illusions in Heeresgruppe G headquarters about the consequences of an Allied landing in southern France. Given the thin dispersion of its forces along the coast, there was little hope that an Allied landing could be stopped. With no reserves but for the 11. Panzer-Division and little likelihood of any additional forces, a significant counterattack seemed improbable. Blaskowitz did discuss some possibilities with his counterpart in northern Italy, Generalfeldmarschall Albert Kesselring. However, Kesselring had his hands full with Allied advances beyond Rome and was attempting to scrape together units to reinforce the Bay of Genoa, an equally plausible Allied amphibious objective. As a result, no reinforcements seemed likely from Italy.

In early August, Heeresgruppe G began planning a withdrawal operation from southern France. The two most likely Allied landing areas were the Bouches-du-Rhône (Mouth of the Rhône) region east of Marseille or the Var coast east of Toulon. General der Infanterie Wiese from AOK 19 was convinced that the latter objective was the most likely. In either case, the primary objective of Heeresgruppe G would be to deny the ports of Toulon and Marseille to the Allies. Blaskowitz knew that 11. Panzer-Division would take at least four days to move from Toulouse to likely landing beaches, and probably longer. Instead of wasting this precious reserve in a futile defense of the ports, Blaskowitz preferred to save it as a mobile rearguard force to cover the inevitable withdrawal of Heeresgruppe G. Withdrawal would require Hitler's permission, so Blaskowitz and his officers attempted to sway senior leaders in the OKW headquarters in Berlin about the benefits of saving the Heeresgruppe G formations to conduct the eventual defense of the German frontier in the Saar, Alsace and Lorraine.

German tactical doctrine favored the use of a strong counterattack against any amphibious landing, and this practice had been followed repeatedly at Sicily, Salerno and Anzio to little avail. Since 1943, Rommel had been advocating a shift of tactics with more reliance on a main line of resistance along the coast. This was forced on the army both by Hitler's infatuation with coastal fortification as well as the meager manpower reserves. The use of coastal fortification seemed a prudent economy of force option, allowing large sectors of coastline to be defended by small numbers of second-rate troops with second-rate weapons. Lacking any mobile reserves, it was a strategy of despair.

Blaskowitz had little confidence that the ports of Toulon and Marseille could be held against a determined Allied attack, and so determined to minimize his losses by restricting the forces committed to the defense of the ports. Instead, he instructed the Kriegsmarine to deny the use of the ports to the Allies by preparing the main facilities for demolition. Critical infrastructure such as cranes and docks were to be blown up and the main channels were to be rendered impassible by scuttling ships across the entrances.

Through early August, German intelligence became increasingly convinced that an invasion of southern France was imminent. Allied bombing raids had intensified along the coast. Rumors were circulating amongst the French that the landings would coincide with the anniversary of Napoleon's return from Elba on August 15. On August 10, the Luftwaffe informed Blaskowitz that Allied troops were embarking in the Algerian ports based on reconnaissance overflights; on August 13 he learned that a substantial convoy of Allied ships had been spotted off the southern coast of Corsica heading north; this was confirmed by another flight on August 14. Allied bombing of the Rhône bridges reinforced this assessment. Indeed, the signs of a forthcoming invasion

seemed so strong that on the afternoon of August 13, Blaskowitz personally contacted the commander of 11. Panzer-Division and instructed him to begin moving his division from Toulouse eastward to the Nîmes–Arles area with the aim of crossing to the east bank of the Rhône River in anticipation of a likely Allied landing in Provence.

ALLIED PLANS

Allied planning for landings in southern France were complicated by the prolonged controversy and indecision over Operation *Anvil*. Detailed planning did not begin until late June when the moribund Operation *Anvil* was reborn as Operation *Dragoon*. Debate over the size of the operation had gradually settled on a three-division landing by the US Army followed by reinforcement by French divisions.

The location of the landing was shaped by the lessons from the recent Anzio campaign. The Wehrmacht had controlled the high ground beyond the beachhead, keeping the Allied forces under continual observation and artillery fire. As a result, *Dragoon* planners sought a location that would enable the landing force quickly to seize the high ground beyond the beachhead to create a firm defensive line. Since the operational objective of the landings was the seizure of the ports of Toulon and Marseille, the planners studied the terrain to the east and west of the ports, as well as the coastline in between the ports. While there were suitable beaches in the Golf-de-Fos east of the ports, the terrain was flat and broken up by the Rhône estuary and swampy areas. La Ciotat Bay between Marseille and Toulon offered some possibilities, but the proximity to the ports as well as the heavy fortification of Ciotat Harbor would have exposed any landing zones to heavy German artillery fire. Much the same was true of the Hyères area, which was within range of the numerous heavy artillery positions on the eastern side of Toulon. The Var coast eventually

German coastal batteries were a considerable worry to Allied planners. A newly installed battery of two powerful Schneider 220mm M17 guns on the heights of Pointe des Issambres south of Saint-Aygulf were an especially grave threat to the landings near Saint-Raphaël, but the guns were disabled by an air strike on August 11. (NARA)

emerged as the most attractive landing site. The coast was not especially well defended yet had several adequate beaches. The high ground of the Maures Massif was within easy range of the beaches, and offered a fine defensive perimeter if the Germans followed their usual practice of launching an immediate counterattack against the beachhead. The plans were imbued with darkly pessimistic and cautious assumptions based on the near-defeats of the Salerno and Anzio landings and were preoccupied with the need to set up a strong defensive perimeter against a strong German counterattack. So, for example, the logistics plans called for large quantities of artillery ammunition to defend the beachhead but relatively modest supplies of gasoline for the first few weeks, which were expected to be relatively static. These planning assumptions would continue to haunt the campaign over the next few weeks when the German attack failed to materialize and the operations suddenly became mobile.

By the summer of 1944, Allied planners had become well practiced in amphibious operations and the *Dragoon* plan showed a high level of sophistication. The amphibious landings would be preceded by an air campaign aimed at isolating the battlefield from German reinforcements by cutting key bridges, especially along the Rhône. In addition, the air campaign would also be directed at softening coastal defenses. To prevent the Germans from determining the precise location of the landings, the air attacks were conducted all along the Mediterranean coast with only about a third of the missions against the actual landing beaches on the Var coast. When Gen. Truscott was assigned command of VI Corps, he made several changes to the plan, most notably shifting his former division, the 3rd, to the vital left flank facing toward Toulon. This would position it to face any German counterattack from the west, or alternately would place it to move rapidly on Toulon if German resistance was weak.

The landings at Utah Beach had shown the value of airborne forces in disrupting German defenses, so *Dragoon* included an airborne landing in the center of the landing zone. The 1st Airborne Task Force was assigned to seize the high ground beyond the beaches to help create the "Blue Line" defensive perimeter.

One problem unique to *Dragoon* was the presence of several substantial islands off the coast on the southern fringe of the landing area that could potentially threaten the landings with artillery fire. These would be eliminated by separate landings of special operations forces: Sitka Force based on the 1st Special Services Force, and the Romeo and Rosie forces based on French commando units.

THE CAMPAIGN

OPENING MOVES

The preliminary air campaign began in early July with missions by the heavy bombers of the 15th Air Force against key rail lines and bridges. Midsummer also saw an escalation in airdrop missions to the Maquis from Algiers. A final bombing plan was released on August 4, and saw an intensification of both heavy and medium bomber strikes. By D-Day, five of the six major Rhône bridges had been cut, rail connections to Lyon had been severely disrupted and both the Luftwaffe and Kriegsmarine had suffered significant losses. The final stage of the bombing plan, Operation *Nutmeg*, struck German coastal batteries and coastal radars. The Allied effort was substantially enhanced by Maquis operations in southern France, a mixture of missions sponsored by SPOC combined with local initiatives. The FFI cut rail lines and destroyed or damaged 32 bridges. FFI infiltration of the French postal and communications network also assisted in cutting German military communications. As a result, more and more German communication was shifted to the radio network, making it far more accessible to Allied signals intelligence. This would have significant effects in the first weeks of the campaign.

The cruiser USS *Philadelphia* opens fire on German coastal defenses during the preliminary bombardment of Delta Beach. (NARA)

Operation *Dragoon*, August 15, 1944

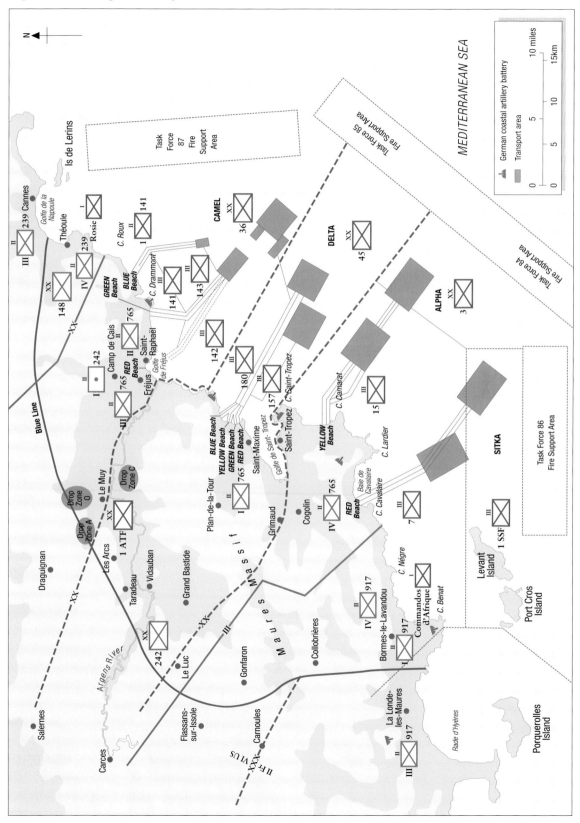

A dedicated deception operation unfolded in the pre-dawn hours of D-Day, August 15, 1944, by Task Group 80.4. Smaller warships, torpedo boats, and gunboats were sent to either flank of the actual invasion beaches to simulate landings. The small flotillas deployed radar reflectors from towed balloons to create the impression of a larger force, and were accompanied by aircraft dropping chaff. A small force of PT boats and other craft made a feint toward Genoa, commanded by Lieutenant-Commander Douglas Fairbanks, the Hollywood star. A force directed by the destroyer USS *Endicott* headed for La Ciotat between Marseille and Toulon while the gunboats HMS *Aphis* and *Scarab* headed to the other side of the landing zone near Antibes and shelled German shore positions as if a landing would follow. The Ciotat deception was reinforced by a fake airborne landing staged by the RAF's 216 Squadron. Around 0400hrs, the five Dakota transports dropped substantial amounts of chaff to simulate a much larger formation, operated Mandril electronic jammers characteristic of earlier Allied airborne operations and then dropped miniature dummy paratroopers and exploding rifle simulators. The deception missions did in fact confuse German commanders, but on the other hand, there were so few mobile reserves that the Wehrmacht had little ability to respond.

SPECIAL FORCES MISSIONS

Rear Admiral L. A. Davidson's Task Force 86 and its associated Special Forces units were assigned to capture the islands off the Provence coast before the invasion to silence coastal batteries stationed there. Sitka Force, consisting of the 1st Special Service Force (1st SSF) and the associated naval Task Unit 86.3 were assigned to seize the islands of Levant and Port-Cros on the southern side of the landing zones. The 2nd and 3rd regiments, 1st SSF, landed on the southeastern side of Levant against no opposition and quickly headed north to deal with the main threat, the heavy artillery battery located at Pointe du Titan. Elements of 3rd/1st SSF quickly overran the site, only to discover the guns were elaborate fakes. The island's garrison, the 18./GR 917, used the old French fortifications and monasteries as resistance points, but were gradually overwhelmed through the rest of August 15, losing about 25 killed and the remaining 110 becoming POWs. The 1st/1st SSF landed on neighboring

Port-Cros and quickly seized the eastern side of the island. The German garrison, 17./GR 917, retreated into the old Fort l'Ecussac where they were impervious to infantry attack. An afternoon fire mission by the cruiser USS *Augusta* proved equally futile, as did an air attack on August 17. The siege was finally broken later on August 17 when the battleship HMS *Ramillies* hammered the fort with 12 rounds from its 15in. guns, prompting the Germans to surrender.

Romeo Force, based on the French commandos d'Afrique, was assigned to land near Cavalière, disable any remaining coastal guns at Cap Nègre and occupy Le Canadel to the east. A preliminary force of 60 commandos landed shortly after midnight but too far west owing to the nighttime haze. They marched to Cap Nègre and cleared the strongpoint. The main force landed as planned and set up roadblocks along the coastal road. Rosie Force conducted a separate mission at Deux Frères Pointe, which went badly from the start when the 67 French marines walked into a minefield a few hundred yards from the landing area. After a few mines detonated, the group was pinned down by the local German garrison and forced to surrender the next morning.

Although the Normandy airborne landings had demonstrated the problems of dropping airborne forces at night given the limitations of the existing navigation technology, the *Dragoon* airborne landings were scheduled for the pre-dawn hours anyway. The usual tactic was to deliver pathfinders to the drop zone before the main landing force to help establish radio beacons and visual signals for the main landings. The operation got off to a bad start when the pathfinder transports discovered that the drop zone was covered with a dense summer fog. The primitive SCR-717 radars proved little help, forcing the pilots to rely on dead reckoning. As a result, of the nine pathfinder teams, only two landed anywhere near their intended target and the rest some eight to 13 miles away.

Mission *Albatross* arrived over the coast after 0400hrs consisting of 396 aircraft divided into ten serials and carrying 5,600 paratroopers and 150 field guns. The first serial from the 442nd Troop Carrier Group (TCG) with elements of the 509th Parachute Infantry Battalion and 463rd Field Artillery Battalion arrived over the DZ-C around 0430hrs but found no navigation aids in place. Hilltops that poked out above the fog provided modest aid in locating DZ-C and two companies of paratroopers and two batteries of 75mm pack howitzers were delivered with surprising accuracy in view of the

LEFT
A patrol from Co. C, 509th Parachute Infantry Battalion, moves down route D47 between La Motte and the crossroad with D25 north of Le Muy on August 15. (NARA)

RIGHT
Saint-Tropez was captured by US paratroopers and the French FFI Brigade des Maures led by Marc Rainaud, seen here being awarded the Silver Star for valor by Lt. Gen. Patch on August 18. (NARA)

LCVPs bring the 15th Infantry ashore with the third wave on Alpha Yellow around 0830hrs from the USS *Samuel Chase* (APA-26) and USS *Andromeda* (AKA-15). The smoke pots deposited by the lead wave are still smoldering in the background. (NARA)

circumstances. The second serial from the 441st Group was confused by clouds off the coast and dumped their 600 paratroopers and howitzers near the coastal town of Saint-Tropez some ten miles from DZ-C. The units that did land accurately in DZ-C had a hard time rounding up their equipment and howitzers owing to the hilly terrain.

Four more serials with the 517th PIR and 460th FAB were dropped over DZ-A starting at 0431hrs. The drops were widely dispersed but about a third of the force landed near enough to the drop zone to assemble and move against their objective. The seventh serial carrying the 3/515th PIR was also off course and dumped its paratroopers near Fayence about 15 miles from the target. The next serial benefited from some improvised lights set up on DZ-A by the paratroopers and delivered a half-dozen pack howitzers close to the target. The final serial to DZ-A scattered the 1/517th PIR several miles away owing to the lingering navigation problems.

The next objective was DZ-O where the British pathfinders had set up Eureka beacons. Although this made a much more concentrated drop possible, still only about 60 percent of the planes managed to deliver their paratroopers accurately. However, this was better than the other drop zones without navigation aids, where only about 40 percent of the paratroopers were delivered to within a mile of their intended landing area.

The glider reinforcements, Mission *Bluebird*, consisted of the 435th TCG with 35 Horsa gliders and the 436th TCG with 40 CG-4A gliders, mainly carrying the British 2nd Para's artillery. Owing to heavy fog lingering over DZ-O, the 435th TCG was ordered to return to base owing to the high fuel consumption when towing the large Horsa. The 436th TCG towing the lighter CG-4A circled over Landing Zone O (LZ-O) for an hour and released 33 gliders with others being lost or forced to return with mechanical problems.

Mission *Bluebird* returned in the afternoon with the 435th TCG delivering 37 Horsa gliders containing 233 troops, 35 jeeps, 30 howitzers and 15 tons of ammunition. The gliders were successfully released over LZ-O starting at 1749hrs. They were followed by Mission *Canary*, a serial of 41 transports of the 437th TCG carrying the 736 troops of the 551st Parachute Battalion. Although ground conditions remained hazy through the day, the late erection of pathfinder navigation aids made the drop about perfect with the battalion beginning to jump at 1804hrs. The largest glider landing of the day, Mission *Dove*, consisted of 335 CG-4A gliders carrying the 55th Glider Infantry Battalion along with support, and was flown by transport groups that had taken part in the earlier missions. In spite of the inevitable complications, about 95 percent of the gliders reached the landing zones starting around 1810hrs. The congestion in the landing zones as well as German anti-glider obstacles proved to be a significant hazard, and many gliders were wrecked in the process with 11 glider pilots killed and 30 injured, and 100 glider troops suffering serious injuries. There was little German resistance in the landing zones.

1st Airborne Task Force, Operation *Dragoon* summary	
Paratroop sorties	444
Waco CG-4A sorties	372
Horsa sorties	36
Total transport sorties	852
Paratroops delivered	6,488
Glider troops delivered	2,611
Total troops delivered	9,099
Artillery delivered	213
Vehicles delivered	221

The daytime glider missions were far more successful than the nighttime paratrooper drops with about 90–95 percent of the glider troops landing in or near the landing zone compared with only about 50 percent of the paratroopers. By the end of the day, Gen. Frederick reported that it had been "a wonderful operation so far." As in the case of the US paratrooper landings near Utah Beach in Normandy, the dispersion of the paratroopers ultimately had beneficial tactical consequences even if delaying the attainment of short-term tactical objectives. By late morning, the 1st ATF was well established in and around Le Muy and had thoroughly disrupted German defenses in the whole area. German defenses in the landing area were weak and scattered, consisting mainly of military police patrols. Aside from headquarters units, the only significant unit based in Le Muy was a horse-drawn transport battalion. German resistance centered around Les Arcs and Le Muy and initial attacks by British paratroopers against Le Muy on the morning of August 15 were rebuffed as were attacks later in the day by the 550th Glider Infantry Battalion. Airborne casualties through the end of D-day were 382 American and 52 British dead, the majority of the casualties owing to the hazards of airborne actions rather than German fire.

STORMING ALPHA

Truscott's favorite, the 3rd Infantry Division, was assigned to land on the southernmost of the beaches since it was expected to face the strongest German counterattacks while at the same time being closest to the prime objectives of Toulon and Marseille. There were two Alpha beaches located on the peninsula south of Saint-Tropez: Alpha Red in Cavalaire Bay was assigned to the 7th Infantry and Alpha Yellow, to the east near Pampellone, to the 15th Infantry. This entire sector from the town of Cavalaire-sur-Mer to Saint-Tropez was defended by the IV. Bataillon of Grenadier Regiment 765 (IV./GR 765)

TOP LEFT

One of the M4A1 DD amphibious tanks of the 756th Tank Battalion was disabled by a mine on Alpha Yellow after having swum ashore; troops of the 15th Infantry wait nearby for orders to move forward. (NARA)

TOP RIGHT

A sergeant of the 15th Infantry, 3rd Division, instructs his squad while awaiting orders to move off Alpha Yellow on D-Day morning. (NARA)

BOTTOM

German prisoners are led away from Saint-Tropez after a combined force of paratroopers and FFI had taken it earlier in the day. (NARA)

The preliminary air and naval bombardment was followed by a minesweeping operation off the coast in the pre-dawn hours. One of the innovations since Normandy was the use of Apex craft to deal with the threat of coastal obstructions. These were radio-controlled LCVPs loaded with high explosive that were designed to blast a hole in the coastal obstacle belts. They were launched against the Alpha beaches around 0715hrs and managed to destroy a number of concrete obstacles off shore. They were followed by rocket-firing craft that were primarily intended to detonate mines on the shore. The landing force was preceded by four amphibious Duplex Drive (DD) M4A1 tanks of the 756th Tank Battalion. A mine sank one while the three surviving tanks parked in shallow water and proceeded to engage targets of opportunity. They were soon followed by 38 LCVPs carrying the 2/7th and 3/7th Infantry, and two of these struck mines resulting in 60 casualties. German resistance consisted of sporadic small-arms fire but the main threat was the large numbers of mines. The Wehrmacht prisoners were mostly Russians, Poles and Turkomen intermingled with a small number of German officers and NCOs. The 7th Infantry's three battalions fanned out in the late morning, spearheaded by special "battle patrols" assigned to specific objectives. The 30th Infantry followed the 7th Infantry on Alpha Red at H+80 minutes.

The landing of the 15th Infantry on Alpha Yellow proceeded in much the same fashion, with DD tanks leading the way. However, the LCVPs proceeded to the beach so fast that they passed the swimming tanks, swamping one of them with their wake. One tank was disabled on the beach by a mine, but there was so little resistance on the beach that the tanks saw little combat. The resistance in this sector was very scattered and consisted mainly of unenthusiastic *Ost* troops who quickly surrendered. The 1/15th Infantry headed for the high ground around the town of Ramatuelle to link up with 30th Infantry while the other two battalions headed toward Saint-Tropez. Earlier in the morning, Cos. B and C of the 509th PIB had been mistakenly parachuted near Saint-Tropez in one of the pre-dawn drops. The paratroopers joined with the French FFI's Brigade des Maures and set off to seize Saint-Tropez, advancing through the town and securing most of it except for a determined German unit in the town's citadel. When the 15th Infantry arrived later in the day, they reinforced the attack on the citadel, which capitulated at 1530hrs. In total, the division captured 1,627 prisoners on D-Day.

TOP LEFT
LST-1164 was part of Wave 8A heading for Alpha Red but it was stopped by concrete beach obstacles on its first two tries. It finally landed at 1145hrs, with an M8 light armored car of C/117th Cavalry landing first followed by a M15 multiple-gun-motor-carriage of the 441st AAA Battalion. (NARA)

TOP RIGHT
German prisoners gather on Yellow Beach to await transfer to ships off the coast. The wreckage in the background is an L-4 Grasshopper (Piper Cub) observation plane that made a forced landing earlier in the morning on the beach. (NARA)

BOTTOM
An M10 3in. GMC of Co. C, 601st Tank Destroyer Battalion heads inland following the landings. (NARA)

IN THE CENTER: DELTA BEACH

Delta Force was made up from the 45th Division and Rear Admiral B. J. Rogers' Task Force 85. Delta Beach was on the opposite side of the Golfe de Saint-Tropez, east of Sainte-Maxime. This sector was defended by I./GR 765 and a single coastal artillery battery. The attack on Delta Red and Delta Green by the 157th Infantry was preceded by four DD tanks; although they safely arrived on the beach, all hit mines and were disabled. A single German 75mm gun fired a few rounds at the incoming LCVPs before being silenced by destroyer fire. Likewise, a trio of 81mm mortars in tobruks on Cap des Sardineaux fired a few rounds before being shelled into silence. The 157th Infantry landed against little resistance and 1/157th Infantry headed five miles inland to Plan-de-la-Tour while the other two battalions fanned out toward

Sainte-Maxime; the 3/157th Infantry took the town by dusk after overcoming resistance in the Hotel du Nord and in the port. The 180th Infantry landed to the right on Delta Yellow and Delta Blue, preceded by eight DD tanks of the 191st Tank Battalion. On the right, the 1/180th landed on Delta Blue with little problem, but encountered significant German resistance as it moved north up the coastal road to Saint-Aygulf, advancing only two miles during the day. In the center, the 2/180th landed on Delta Yellow and pushed westward into the Maures hills about four miles. On the left, the 3/180th landed on Delta Blue and headed to the high ground north of the beach. A platoon of the division's 45th Reconnaissance Troop set off by jeep along the D-25 road and met up with paratroopers of the 509th PIB later in the day. The division's third regiment, the 179th Infantry, landed later in the day and was put in reserve near Sainte-Maxime. With the road toward Le Muy open according to the jeep patrol, the 191st Tank Battalion sent a patrol to Le Muy where they helped the paratroopers overcome the last defenders in the town late in the afternoon.

DISASTER AVERTED: CAMEL BEACH

Camel Force, consisting of the 36th Division and Rear Admiral Spencer Lewis's Task Force 87, was assigned Camel Beach in the Golfe de Fréjus on either side of the port of Saint-Raphaël. This sector was guarded by unusually strong German defenses compared with the other *Dragoon* landing beaches. This was not altogether surprising as Fréjus was a traditional invasion point since antiquity; Julius Caesar had landed there to initiate his conquest of Gaul and Napoleon had picked the same spot on his return from exile on Elba. German coastal defense doctrine emphasized the protection of ports and this area contained not only the port of Saint-Raphaël, but also a flat beach leading into the Argens river valley, which offered a direct route to Le Muy and Draguignan beyond. The Italian Fourth Army had recognized the significance of this location when they had occupied the area in 1940–43, and had positioned six batteries with two dozen Ansaldo 149/19 149mm field howitzers in the heights around the port. After the 1943 armistice, these remained in service with volunteer Italian crews as "Abteilung Coniglio," named after their commander. By 1944, these had been redesignated and the three batteries west of Fréjus became I./HAA 671 (mot.) while the three emplaced batteries northeast of Fréjus became I./HAA 1192. In the weeks prior to the landings, the Kriegsmarine had begun to install a battery of the old but powerful Schneider M17 220mm guns on the Pointe des Issambres south of Saint-Aygulf but these were disabled by a US bombing raid on August 11 before they became fully operational. The 11./HKAR 1291 was deployed in Saint-Aygulf in Strongpoint Geranie with four French 75mm guns in H671 casemates. Further to the east, the Kreigsmarine had three 150mm destroyer guns near Cap du Dramont, installed in M272 bunkers. Nearby, the Luftwaffe had installed Flak Abt. 481 in several batteries around Anthéor with over a dozen 88mm Flak 18 guns.

An M10 3in. GMC of the 636th Tank destroyer Battalion comes ashore on the narrow and rock-strewn Green Beach with LST-49 in the background. This beach was dubbed "Quarry Beach" by the 36th Division because of the nearby quarry. (NARA)

Engineers supporting the 143rd Infantry cross a fortified bridge on the western side of Saint-Raphaël on the morning of August 16 with Notre Dame de la Victoire in the background. (NARA)

Besides the substantial artillery defenses, the Golfe de Fréjus was heavily fortified and organized as Stützpunkt Gruppe (Strongpoint Group) Saint-Raphaël with four strongpoints. Each of these was in turn made up of two or three resistance nests (*Widerstandsnester*), which were clusters of bunkers usually a platoon in strength with more machine guns, mortars, and light guns than a normal infantry formation. These defenses were occupied principally by II./GR 765 and parts of III./GR 765 with the rest of the battalion in reserve around Fréjus. In addition, Panzerjäger Bn. 1038 with towed 88mm anti-tank guns reinforced the army defenses. The coastline to the northeast of Saint-Raphaël was defended by IV./GR 239, an *Ost* battalion of the 148. Infanterie-Division.

The 141st Infantry was assigned Camel Green and Camel Blue on the division's right, an important task since it would constitute the right shoulder of the entire invasion area. These beaches were away from the German fortified zone, though still within range of much of the artillery. The attack was preceded by eight M4A1 DD amphibious tanks of the 753rd Tank Battalion, but they were launched from 4,000 yards off shore and so arrived after the first wave of LCVPs. There was some small-arms fire at first, but the *Osttruppen* of IV./GR 239 did not have any enthusiasm for fighting and began surrendering in large numbers. The main threat to the beach came from the abundant German artillery, but, without forward observers, it was not especially accurate. The regiment's main mission was to secure the Agay roadstead and the heights of the Massif de l'Esterel beyond. The 143rd Infantry quickly followed the 141st Infantry on Camel Green, and was assigned to move westward against Saint-Raphaël. The advance of 2/143rd Infantry ground to a halt by late afternoon after running into the bunkers of Stützpunkt Löwe on the eastern approaches to Saint-Raphaël.

Unlike the other beaches, the 36th Division's third regiment, the 142nd Infantry, was scheduled to land in the afternoon after the 143rd Infantry had already begun to move into Saint-Raphaël from the east. Camel Red Beach was a potential deathtrap, in the center of the kill zone of the Saint-Raphaël strongpoint group. At 1100hrs, US Navy minesweepers attempting to clear the deep-water channel leading into the port were heavily shelled by German

AMERICAN UNITS

36th Division Maj. Gen. John Dahlquist

A	Task Force Abbott
B	Task Force Bishop
C	Task Force Cardinal

141st Infantry Regiment

D	Recon Company
E	1/141st Infantry
F	A/141st Infantry
G	B/141st Infantry
H	C/141st Infantry
I	2/141st Infantry
J	E/141st Infantry
K	F/141st Infantry
L	G/141st Infantry
M	3/141st Infantry

142nd Infantry Regiment

N	1/142nd Infantry
O	2/142nd Infantry
P	3/142nd Infantry

143rd Infantry Regiment

Q	1/143rd Infantry
R	A/143rd Infantry
S	B/143rd Infantry
T	C/143rd Infantry
U	2/143rd Infantry
V	E/143rd Infantry
W	F/143rd Infantry
X	G/143rd Infantry
Y	3/143rd Infantry
Z	I/143rd Infantry
AA	K/143rd Infantry
AB	L/143rd Infantry

EVENTS

1 Coastal artillery batteries such as 14./HKAR 1291 on the heights over Les Issambres are bombed by Allied aircraft in the preparatory phase of the operation.

2 The 2 and 3/141st Infantry Regiment land against little opposition on Camel Green Beach at 0800hrs and immediately begin to move off the beach. The 1/143rd Infantry follows at 0945hrs, 2/143rd at 1000hrs and 3/143rd at 1035hrs.

3 The 3rd Battalion of the 141st Infantry lands on the narrow Camel Blue Beach against little opposition.

4 Naval gunfire silences 5./MAA 627 near Anthéor and 1/141st Infantry clears elements of Ost Bataillon 661 from Stützpunkt Wiesel by mid-morning.

5 Co. G, 2/141st Infantry, clears Cap Dramont by 1000hrs and then proceeds to clear out Stützpunkt Steinbock on the western side of Agay Bay.

6 Co. A, 1/141st Infantry, clears out Stützpunkt Bär on the east side of Agay Bay and then proceeds to link up with the lead elements from 2/141st Infantry.

7 Cos. A and B, 1/141st Infantry, approach German positions on the hill overlooking Anthéor from the rear and overwhelm the garrison, capturing 47 prisoners.

8 Co. E, 143rd Infantry, heads along the coast road toward Saint-Raphaël, skirmishing with a German roadblock near Boulouris.

9 Having cleared Camel Green, the 143rd Infantry sets out in battalion columns to clear Saint-Raphaël. The northernmost column from 1/143rd Infantry skirmishes with a German position on Hill 120 around midday before proceeding for Saint-Raphaël's eastern suburbs.

10 Co. G, 143rd Infantry, becomes entangled in the Germans defenses of Stützpunkt Löwe on the southeastern side of Saint-Raphaël. Part of the company deals with the pillboxes while other platoons head back toward Boulouris to help Co. E.

11 US Navy minesweepers head into Saint-Raphaël harbor in early afternoon to clear a path to Camel Red Beach. Intense artillery fire from coastal batteries and bunkers force the ships to retire. The US Air Force sends in 93 B-24 bombers to soften the defenses. The Navy follows with gunfire, 12 Apex drones and rocket craft.

12 When the 142nd Infantry approaches Camel Red Beach at Z-Hour (1500hrs), the German fire is still so intense that the Navy Beach Assault Commander decides to change plans and land the regiment on Camel Green Beach instead. The landing on Camel Green Beach starting at 1532hrs.

13 Co. I, 143rd Infantry, swings north of Saint-Raphaël and clears German defenses. Late in the day, 1/143rd Infantry pushes through with plans to clear Saint-Raphaël the following day.

14 Cos. K and L, 143rd Infantry, reach the outskirts of Saint-Raphaël by the early evening of August 15, but wait until the following morning before pushing through the town, supported by the 1/143rd Infantry.

15 With the 143rd Infantry clearing Saint-Raphaël and Frejus, on the morning of August 16 the 142nd Infantry begins to push toward the valleys north of the towns.

The most intense fighting of the day takes place around Camp Gallieni.

16 Having cleared Frejus by mid-afternoon, the 143rd Infantry begins pushing north to link up with 142rd Infantry.

17 The last major German resistance in the towns is overcome near Camp de Cais around 1730hrs, and units begin moving north into the Esterel Forest in hastily formed task forces to reach the "Blue Line" and the 1st Airborne Task Force.

18 Co. B, 143rd Infantry, heads up the Valion Valley around dusk before finally halting for the night after encountering a German roadblock.

19 The three companies of 1/141st Infantry head up the coastal road toward Cannes around noon on August 15.

20 Through the afternoon of August 15, elements of 2/141st Infantry head inland to the Anthéor Plateau through the Grenouillet Ravine.

ARGENS RIVER

SAINT-RAPHAËL

SAINT-AYGULF

LES ISSAMBRES

Beach 264A
Camel Red

142

143

AMPHIBIOUS ASSAULT ON CAMEL BEACH, AUGUST 15, 1944

The US 36th Division spearheads the landings on the French Mediterranean coast

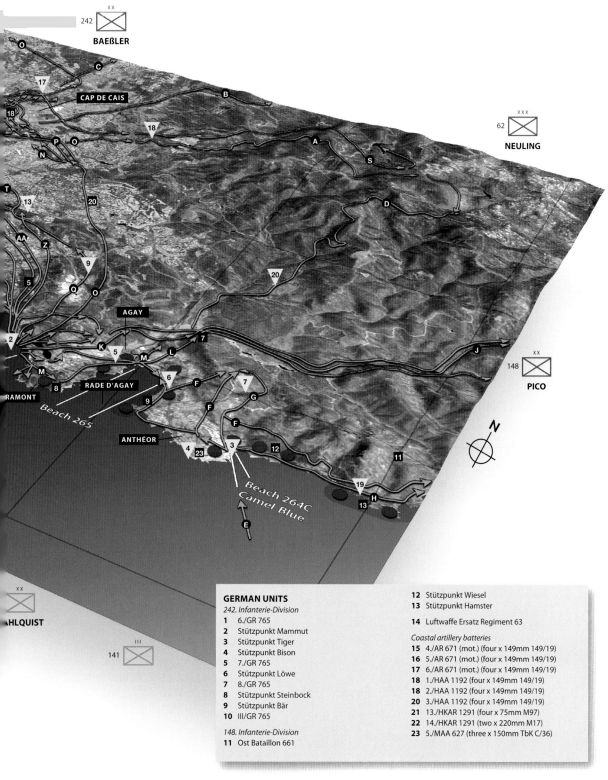

242 ⊠ ××
BAEßLER

62 ⊠ ×××
NEULING

148 ⊠ ××
PICO

CAP DE CAIS

AGAY

RADE D'AGAY

Beach 265

ANTHÉOR

RAMONT

Beach 264C
Camel Blue

⊠ ××
AHLQUIST

141 ⊠ ∣∣∣

GERMAN UNITS
242. Infanterie-Division
1   6./GR 765
2   Stützpunkt Mammut
3   Stützpunkt Tiger
4   Stützpunkt Bison
5   7./GR 765
6   Stützpunkt Löwe
7   8./GR 765
8   Stützpunkt Steinbock
9   Stützpunkt Bär
10 III/GR 765

148. Infanterie-Division
11 Ost Bataillon 661

12 Stützpunkt Wiesel
13 Stützpunkt Hamster

14 Luftwaffe Ersatz Regiment 63

Coastal artillery batteries
15 4./AR 671 (mot.) (four x 149mm 149/19)
16 5./AR 671 (mot.) (four x 149mm 149/19)
17 6./AR 671 (mot.) (four x 149mm 149/19)
18 1./HAA 1192 (four x 149mm 149/19)
18 2./HAA 1192 (four x 149mm 149/19)
20 3./HAA 1192 (four x 149mm 149/19)
21 13./HKAR 1291 (four x 75mm M97)
22 14./HKAR 1291 (two x 220mm M17)
23 5./MAA 627 (three x 150mm TbK C/36)

Avoided on D-Day, Camel Red Beach was later used by Task Group 87.10 for picking up prisoners and wounded. Saint-Raphaël is evident in the background behind the LCTs. (NARA)

shore defenses and artillery and forced to retire. Ninety B-24 bombers dropped 200 tons of bombs into the Camel Red sector shortly after noon to suppress the strongpoint, but when the minesweepers returned around 1235hrs, they still faced heavy fire. Apex drones were sent toward shore in hopes of blowing up beach defenses but most went haywire and some had to be sunk by destroyers when they veered back out to sea toward the fleet. A naval bombardment of the coast followed, but when the landing force reached to within 3,000 yards of shore around 1400hrs, German artillery fire remained intense. Captain Leo Schulten (USN) leading the Camel Red assault group decided to temporarily halt the attack and contacted Admiral Lewis. After attempts to reach the 36th Division headquarters ashore failed, Lewis decided to land the 142nd Infantry on Camel Green and avoid Camel Red. As a result, the 142nd Infantry went ashore at 1515hrs, avoiding a repeat of "Bloody Omaha" that had occurred during the Normandy landings two months before. It was to the credit of the experienced navy–army team that instructions were not blindly followed and so tragedy was averted. Truscott later complained about the delays imposed by the change of plans, but was ignorant of the extent of German defenses. The only major casualties suffered by Camel Force came later in the evening during a Luftwaffe raid. A Do-217 bomber hit LST-282 with an Hs.293 anti-ship missile, sinking it in shallow water and causing 40 casualties.

Allied casualties on D-Day have never been carefully tabulated owing to incomplete records, but were extremely light, about 95 killed and 385 wounded.

THE GERMAN REACTION

Word of the Allied landings began to filter into Heeresgruppe G and AOK 19 headquarters in the pre-dawn hours of August 15. There was still some confusion regarding the focus of attack, partly due to the deception operations around La Ciotat. The FFI actions against German communication networks cut off AOK 19 from Heeresgruppe G after 0800hrs, and Wiese initially had to rely on intelligence reports coming out of the neighboring OB Südwest in Italy. Heeresgruppe G information mainly came through OB West

headquarters near Paris. Communications with Neuling's 62. AK headquarters in Draguignan were cut almost immediately when Allied paratroopers landed in Le Muy, six miles to the south. The attack provided Blaskowitz with the pretext to begin moving units in the western coastal sectors away from the coast and toward the Rhône Valley for an eventual withdrawal. This could be explained to Berlin as preparations for a counterattack. Blaskowitz shifted his headquarters to Avignon as part of this process.

Since there were no reserves in the 62. AK sector, Blaskowitz had to rely on forces further west. The 338. Infanterie-Division was already in the process of pulling out of Bouches-du-Rhône for Paris so Blaskowitz ordered the division to halt its movement. He instructed the 189. Infanterie-Division commander, General-Major Richard von Schwerin to create a *Kampfgruppe* (battlegroup) to counterattack the beachhead using a mishmash of units cobbled up from divisions in the area. The battlegroup was to assemble in the Vidauban area, then attack the Allied airborne forces near Le Muy and relieve the trapped 62. AK headquarters in Draguignan. By the end of August 15, Schwerin had little more than a partial infantry regiment at his disposal, and plans had been expanded from a relief of the 62. AK headquarters to an unrealistic scheme to counterattack on the Fréjus–Saint-Raphaël beachhead after the paratroopers had been overcome.

By the morning of August 16, Schwerin had assembled a *Kampfgruppe* of four infantry battalions and at 0700hrs, it began moving toward Le Muy, pushing a paratrooper outpost from Les Arcs around 0730hrs. Within a few hours, the 517th Parachute Infantry were reinforced by the arrival of 2/180th Infantry from the beachhead, supported by a platoon of M10 tank destroyers of the 645th Tank Destroyer Battalion. The US columns advancing out of the Saint-Raphaël beachhead cut across the roads behind Schwerin's troops in Les Arcs. Fighting through the day surrounded Les Arcs and after dark, Schwerin ordered his forces to escape under the cover of darkness, having lost half their men and most of their heavy equipment. It was the only significant German counterattack of the beachhead and fizzled out before it built up any momentum. By noon on August 17, the 36th Division arrived around Le Muy in full strength, relieving the 1st Airborne Task Force.

D+1 was spent expanding the beachhead toward the "Blue Line," the main defensive position on the heights of Massif des Maures to shelter the landings from an anticipated German counterattack. The heaviest fighting on August 16 was in Fréjus–Saint-Raphaël where the 36th Division spent much of the day overcoming the significant German defenses in the

LEFT
The Luftwaffe staged small-scale bomb and missile attacks on the fleet, usually at dusk and dawn when cloud cover offered some protection. This kept the fleet's anti-aircraft gunners alert and nervous. (NARA)

RIGHT
The Wehrmacht attempted to withdraw its three railroad artillery batteries from southern France, but most were damaged by air attack or caught in the Montélimar area. This is a Schneider 274mm Mle 1917 of Eisenbahnbatterie 692 damaged by Allied air attack and left near La Coucourde in late August 1944. (NARA)

VIKING SWANSONG (pp. 52–53)

Kampfgeschwader 100 "Wiking" (KG 100) was the Luftwaffe's specialist with revolutionary guided anti-ship weapons, including the Fritz-X guided bomb and Hs.293 guided missile. They saw their shocking debut in the Mediterranean theater in 1943–44 against the Allied fleet off Salerno and Anzio, sinking the Italian battleship *Roma* and a number of American and British warships. Following the D-Day landings in June 1944, they were reoriented from their bases in southern France to take part in desperate and costly attacks against Allied shipping and key bridges in Normandy. By 1944, the Allied navies had developed electronic jamming systems to interfere with their radio command guidance signals, and during Operation *Dragoon* 22 Allied ships were fitted with anti-missile jammers. KG100 operated both the Do-217 medium bomber and He-177 heavy bomber but the end of Do-217 production in May 1944 led to the consolidation of surviving aircraft of this type into III Gruppe (III./KG 100). So in August 1944, III./KG 100 had a motley assortment of older Do-217E-5 (Hs.293) as well as the improved extended-wing versions including the Do-217K-2 Fritz-X carrier and the Do-217K-3 and M-11, which could launch either type of weapon. The Do-217K-3 seen here **(1)** had five missile hard-points, but they usually carried only one missile on the starboard wing because only a single missile could be guided at one time. If a second missile was carried on the port wing, the bomber was very difficult to fly owing to both the

weight imbalance and drag when the first missile was launched. Instead, the other hard-point usually carried a spare fuel tank that was dropped simultaneously with the missile.

In August 1944, III./KG 100 was commanded by Hauptmann Heinrich Schmetz and was based at Francazal near Toulouse. It had already lost a dozen aircraft in the first two weeks of August during attacks on key bridges in Normandy and anti-shipping missions off the Gironde estuary and there were only 14 bombers operational on August 15 when attacks began on the *Dragoon* fleet. The first attack as seen here was launched around 1830hrs against the ships off Saint-Raphaël on August 15 **(2)**. By now, III./KG 100 was well aware of the Allied jammers and had developed new tactics to circumvent them. Instead of the usual practice of guiding the missile on a path perpendicular to launch, the Do-217 instead continued toward the target with their radio guidance signals burning through the jamming signals. While this overcame the Allied countermeasures, such tactics placed a heavy burden on the missile operator adjacent the pilot, and only one hit was scored in three days of attacks, with LST-282 succumbing to an Hs.293 **(3)** strike from Oberfeldwebel Kube's aircraft on the evening of August 15. Two Do-217s were lost the first night of the attacks and a half-dozen more over the next few days of attacks. In ten weeks of fighting from D-Day June 6, 1944, III./KG 100 suffered 100 percent crew casualties and was disbanded in mid-September.

towns. The 148. Infanterie-Division in the Cannes area sent a battalion to counterattack the beachhead, but was overrun by the 2/141st Infantry who were rapidly moving up the coast toward La Napoule. The first elements of French II Corps, CC1 under Sudré, were already disembarking.

By the night of August 16/17, Heeresgruppe G was in a quandary over its options. Detailed information about the Allied landings was poor as the units along the coast had largely vanished, or their communication lines had been cut; the Luftwaffe was incapable of conducting reconnaissance over the beachhead. The movement of reinforcements to the east side of the Rhône including 11. Panzer-Division had proven extremely difficult both owing to the thorough Allied destruction of major bridges, as well as the presence of Allied aircraft, which mercilessly strafed and bombed any moving column. The countryside was alive with Maquis who made movement difficult even under the cover of darkness.

In Berlin, the situation appeared ominous. In Normandy, AOK 7 and Panzergruppe West were almost completely encircled in the Falaise Pocket. Patton's Third Army was racing along the Loire Valley and appeared to be ready to leapfrog the Seine River on either side of Paris with no appreciable forces to stop them. The landings in southern France threatened to cut off both AOK 1 and 19 unless prompt action was taken. Blaskowitz's plan from earlier in August to withdraw Heeresgruppe G toward Dijon was now treated more seriously. At a briefing with Hitler on August 16, OKW (Oberkommando Wehrmacht) offered the stark choice of withdrawing both Heeresgruppen B and G immediately or risking the destruction of both, leaving the German frontier in the west unguarded. In complete contrast to his previous insistence on the Wehrmacht holding territory "to the last man," Hitler agreed to the OKW plan. This decision essentially conceded two-thirds of France to the Allies without a fight. Hitler insisted that the garrisons of several fortified ports remained to keep them out of Allied hands. Historians have paid little attention to this momentous decision, and Hitler's rationale for the change of heart remains obscure.

At 0940hrs on August 17, Berlin sent the first part of the message to Admiral-Atlantik since the naval communications network was the only one reliably functioning; Blaskowitz didn't receive it until 1115hrs. The instructions stated that all German forces from all branches in Heeresgruppe G west of Orléans–Clermont Ferrand–Montpellier, except for fortress troops and those of AOK 19 already in combat, were immediately to withdraw behind a new defensive line of the Seine–Yonne–Canal de Bourgogne. Late that afternoon at 1730hrs, the order was amplified, instructing OB West that owing to the threat of entrapment, AOK 19, except for forces in Toulon and Marseille, was to withdraw northward to join up with Heeresgruppe B and establish a new defensive line from Sens through Dijon to the Swiss frontier. The eastern elements of 62. AK including 148. and 159. Reserve-Divisionen were to withdraw once pressed into the French–Italian Alps and connect with OB Südwest in Italy to prevent the *Dragoon* force from spilling into Italy and cutting off the Wehrmacht forces north of Rome. This later instruction would have dire consequences over the next few weeks as it created a vacuum to the east of the Rhône escape route. Wehrmacht communications were so bad that Blaskowitz didn't receive the second order until 1100hrs on August 18. The Allied Ultra signals intelligence service sent a decrypt of the message to senior Allied commanders that afternoon, meaning that Patch and Truscott learned of the withdrawal orders almost as soon as Wiese and AOK 19.

The Rhône triangle, August 20–25, 1944

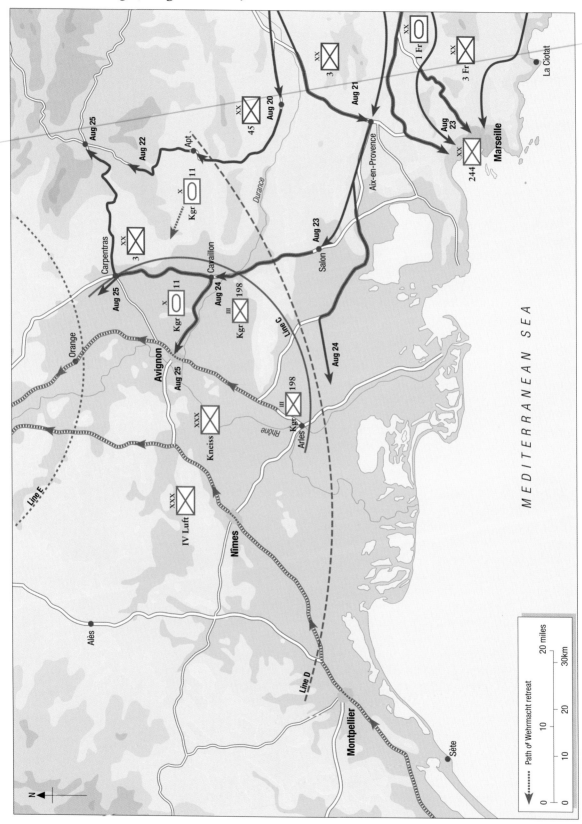

Truscott's VI Corps continued to push out beyond the Blue Line on August 17, with little appreciable resistance. Wiese's plans to establish a new defense line were undermined by the rapidity of the American advance and the paucity of forces at his disposal. Wiese ordered Gen.Lt. Baptist Kneiss's 85. AK to take over command of the Toulon–Marseille sector since 62. AK was effectively surrounded in Draguignan, with the two amalgamated corps now becoming Korps Kneiss. General der Infanterie Neuling and his 62. AK staff were captured while trying to escape on the afternoon of August 18. Korps Kneiss included 244. Infanterie-Division in the Marseille area, elements of 338. Infanterie-Division already assembled by Schwerin during the futile counterattack attempt, and elements of 198. Infanterie-Division trying to cross the Rhône. Generalleutnant Johannes Baeßler was ordered to establish a defense line west of Toulon with whatever was left of 242. Infanterie-Division. Wiese realized that he had to hold Route 7 from Brignoles toward Aix-en-Provence to shield the Rhône River crossings of 11. Panzer-Division and his infantry divisions. However, the complete lack of mobility of the static divisions along the coast and the rapidity of the US Army soon thwarted his plans. A *Kampfgruppe* from 11. Panzer-Division sallied toward Aix on August 18, but it was little more than a feint intended to panic the VI Corps spearheads. The US infantry divisions, though not motorized, had become experienced in motorizing one battalion in each regiment by assigning it all available trucks and attached tank and tank destroyer units to provide temporary lift. The 30th Infantry, 3rd Division, liberated Brignoles by the morning of August 19 while the 179th Infantry, 45th Division, reached Barjols later in the day before Kneiss could establish any cohesive defense in this sector. The VI Corps advance was threatening to complete the envelopment of Toulon and Marseille from the north while at the same time reaching the access points to the Rhône River valley – the escape route for much of Heeresgruppe G.

To add to the German misery, Truscott had dispatched his mobile exploitation force, Task Force Butler, to push north beyond Draguignan on the morning of August 18. French officers who had visited the area a few weeks before the landings insisted that German defenses there were minimal and that the FFI was extremely active. This proved to be the case, as the 117th CRSM in the lead of TF Butler was soon over the Verdon River into the Basses-Alpes (lower Alps) and heading toward the department seat in Digne. The German military police forces in the district under Generalmajor Hans Schuberth of VS 792 were scattered and demoralized after months of fighting with the local Maquis; they had been out of communication with higher headquarters since August 14. The II./Sicherungs Rgt. 194 attempted to reinforce Digne but the FFI downed two bridges, blocking their advance. The German garrison was unwilling to surrender to the Maquis in view of the emnity built up over the past two years of brutal occupation, but Schuberth was willing to capitulate and the Digne garrison of 400 troops surrendered to TF Butler on the evening of August 18. The American unit continued to race northward, aided from department to department by the local FFI units.

The next major objective, Grenoble, was headquarters to 157. Reserve-Division, which had spent most of the previous summer months battling the Maquis in the local mountains. The division was scattered with one regiment in the Grenoble area, one in Gap and the third in Aix-les-Bains providing little opportunity for concerted defense. Generalleutnant Karl Pflaum received contradictory instructions; AOK 19 told him to hold Grenoble until August

The 117th Cavalry Reconnaissance Squadron was in the vanguard of TF Butler, and sent north toward Grenoble. Its jeeps and M8 armored cars are seen crossing the Maire River south of Moustiers-Sainte-Marie in the Alpes-Maritimes on August 18. (NARA)

30 to guard the east flank of forces retreating up the Rhône Valley, while OB Südwest in Italy told him to withdraw his unit into the passes on the French–Italian frontier to prevent any American advance into Italy. With TF Butler closing in, Pflaum decided that the Alps mission was more prudent and he evacuated the city by midnight of August 21. Small elements of TF Butler, the 143rd Infantry and FFI units entered Grenoble on August 22 though fighting continued nearby as scattered German units withdrew into the Alps to the east. Pflaum's decision created a major defensive void to the east flank of Heeresgruppe G's retreat up the Rhône Valley.

PLANS REASSESSED

Hitler's withdrawal orders of August 17 led to a continuing reconsideration of plans by both sides. Blaskowitz was relieved that Hitler and OKW in Berlin had finally come to their senses and authorized a general withdrawal. Had they done so earlier in the month, Heeresgruppe G could have established a defensive line around Dijon in good order. Now, Heeresgruppe G would face the challenge of staging a complicated withdrawal in the face of attack from the air and pursuit on the ground. The 242. Infanterie-Division in Toulon and 244. Infanterie-Division in Marseille would be sacrificed to buy time for the rest of AOK 19 to withdraw up the Rhône. Blaskowitz attempted to establish successive defense lines to be held by the 11. Panzer-Division and 198. Infanterie-Division, and the last three are shown here on the accompanying map (page 56). Reports of American forces beyond the Durance on August 19 were viewed with alarm, but the neither the size nor direction of TF Butler were yet known to German commanders.

On the evening of August 18, Lt. Gen. Patch met with Lt. Gen. Devers to discuss the import of the decrypted German messages and determine future courses of action. Prior to the receipt of the Hitler retreat orders, Patch and Truscott were focused on repelling an anticipated German counterattack; the Ultra decrypt indicated that the Wehrmacht had abandoned any plans for a major counterattack and were instead intent on withdrawing up the Rhône Valley as quickly as possible. On the one hand, VI Corps commander

As the Wehrmacht in the Var department evaporated under the combined impact of the Allied invasion and FFI attacks, the road to Grenoble lay open to a rapid advance by TF Butler. Here, US troops enter the city on August 20. (NARA)

Truscott pleaded with Patch to let him use the French CC1 (Sudré) armored force to help prosecute the campaign toward the Rhône. On the other hand, Gén. de Lattre was arguing with Patch and Devers about the dangers of nibbling away at the elements of the French II Corps as they arrived on the beachhead, insisting that the French force remain intact for their main mission against Toulon and Marseille. The unexpected rapidity of the advance out of the beachhead has already causing logistical problems, and Patch was well aware of the primacy of the capture of the ports. Although there had been plans to dispatch de Lattre's Moroccan mountain troops to seal the Alpine passes toward Italy, Patch decided instead to detach the lightly armed 1st Airborne Task Force and 1st Special Service Force knowing full well from Ultra decrypts that the Germans were in full retreat into Italy. This resulted in the "Champagne Campaign" with the paratroopers proceeding to liberate the resort towns of the Riviera. It took a few days for Patch and Truscott to appreciate fully the opportunity that had been handed them by the withdrawal of 157. Reserve-Division from Grenoble. With this area essentially empty of German troops, it would allow an attack on the flank of the Wehrmacht retreat up the Rhône Valley. However, it would require far more force than the modest TF Butler operating in the area.

LIBERATION OF THE PORTS

The original plans to capture Toulon and Marseille by de Lattre's Army B envisioned a sequential operation against Toulon and then Marseille. The evident German chaos and the US VI Corps' rapid penetration along Route 7 would allow de Lattre to envelop both ports from the north. The 1ère DMI and the 3e DIA began arriving on August 16 along with armored combat commands of the 1ère DB followed by the 9e DIC on August 18. De Lattre organized his forces into five tactical groups, breaking up the armor of the 1ère DB into its constituent combat commands to help reinforce the infantry divisions.

A French M5 half-track moves west from the landing beaches near Sainte-Maxime on August 20 past a wrecked Luftwaffe truck. (NARA)

The first task was to deal with the large concentration of German forces in Hyères, a fortified port to the east of Toulon which had a substantial number of coastal fortifications and several large concentrations of artillery. The town was held by the *Ost* battalion of GR 918 made up mostly of Armenian troops. A French regimental combat team of the 1ère DMI began the attack on Hyères on August 19 while at the same time, 9e DIC moved along Route 7 from the north to seal off the town by seizing towns to the northwest including Solliès-Pont. The resistance in Hyères centered around the Golf Hotel, which was finally taken in the early evening of August 21. Allied warships bombarded the port area south of the town including Giens and the island of Porquerolles. About 180 Armenian troops surrendered on Porquerolles and were evacuated by the USS *Eberle*; bombardment of 150 German troops of III./GR 918 in the old fortifications continued until 1130hrs on August 22 when the garrison hoisted the white flag. Likewise, the coastal battery of the Kriegsmarine MAA 627 on Cap de l'Esterel remained active in spite of continual naval bombardment, not surrendering until August 23.

THE LIBERATION OF TOULON

The envelopment of Toulon was undertaken by 3e DIA on August 19 while the other two infantry divisions were still busy with Hyères and Solliès-Pont. Toulon is in the cusp of mountainous outcroppings both north and south, with Mont Faron to the north of the city. The port was heavily defended by coastal batteries, but these had very limited value in the ensuing campaign as those guns in casemates were limited to a seaward firing arc when the attack came from the landward side. Evacuation of women auxiliaries and U-boat crews had begun on August 13, reducing the size of the garrison to about 18,000, which included about 5,500 naval troops and 2,800 Luftwaffe troops. The 242. Infanterie-Division had a single regiment in the area, GR 918, but it was

Mont Faron shielded Toulon from the north and was studded by old French forts that had been reinforced by the Wehrmacht. This is the Fort de la Croix Faron, built in 1872–75 and captured in 1944 by the Battalion du Choc. (NARA)

scattered from the southwestern suburbs to the east of Hyères and two of its battalions had been lost in the fighting there. The divisional commander, Gen.Lt. Johannes Baeßler was trapped in the divisional headquarters in Hyères, so command of Toulon was handed over to Vize Admiral Heinrich Ruhfus on August 18. Grenadier-Regiment 918 attempted to set up a perimeter defense north of the port in the foothills of Le Coudon and Mont Faron. Three French columns moved on Toulon from the north. These mountains had been heavily fortified for centuries with substantial stone fortresses. There was heavy fighting for the forts of Le Coudon by the commandos and on Mont Faron by the Battalion du Choc of 3e DIA for much of August 22–23. By the end of August 23, the hill forts north of the city had been overcome and the port enveloped on three sides, with the commandos and 3e DIA reinforced by elements of the two infantry divisions previously engaged in clearing Hyères.

The German Army defenses in Toulon were centered around the old bastions of Sainte-Catherine, d'Artigues, de Malbousquet and Lamague, with the caves of the La Poudrière (powder magazine) serving as a staging area. The Kriegsmarine had a number of batteries on the Saint-Mandrier Peninsula that shielded the port on the southwest side. The army and navy headquarters were in the northeast suburb of La Vallette, but the approach of the French troops led V.Adm. Ruhfus to switch his command post to the Saint-Mandrier Peninsula after dark on August 21. The continual fire from the gun batteries on the Saint-Mandrier Peninsula attracted the attention of Allied aircraft and warships. Bomber raids began in earnest on August 18, and the following day, warships of the Western Task Force joined them. The French warships *Fantasque* and *Georges Leygues* were both hit during these engagements, but by August 21 the volume of German fire subsided as more and more of the batteries were demolished.

By the afternoon of August 23, French troops had reached the center of the city and forced the surrender of the Le Mourillon arsenal. The following day saw the gradual capitulation of the bastions and forts with the Arsenal Maritime surrendering at 0900hrs, Fort Sainte-Catherine at 1000hrs and Fort Saint-Louis at 1300hrs, with more than 2,000 prisoners taken that day. Although most of the city proper was taken by the end of the day, there were still substantial German defenses in the port area, on the Saint-Mandrier

This view from the Croix Faron road to the southwest overlooks Toulon with Fort Faron immediately below. The peninsula emanating from the city in the upper center was protected by Fort Saint-Louis at its tip. The Saint-Mandrier Peninsula in the upper left seems disconnected from the mainland as the narrow causeway is hidden in the mist and glare. The high ground in the upper right is the Cap Sicié Peninsula. (NARA)

Peninsula and on the Sicié Peninsula to the southwest. Fighting on August 25 and 26 cleared most of the Sicié Peninsula, leaving only the naval fortifications on the Saint-Mandrier Peninsula. Fighting by the 9e DIC continued until the late afternoon of August 27 when a temporary ceasefire was announced to conduct surrender negotiations. By this time, the heights of Saint-Mandrier were a lunar landscape from the intense bombardment. Vize Admiral Ruhfus surrendered the remaining 1,800 troops in the Saint-Mandrier garrison at 0600hrs on August 28. The fighting for Toulon had cost the French 2,700 dead and wounded while the Wehrmacht had lost 17,000 prisoners and a few thousand killed. Allied planning anticipated it would fall by D+20 but the liberation occurred a week earlier than expected on D+13. German naval engineer teams had demolished the harbor, though not as thoroughly as Naples the year before. American forces began an immediate program to rehabilitate the port, but the emphasis fell on Marseille, with Toulon earmarked for civil commerce.

THE LIBERATION OF MARSEILLE

Although most of the 3e DIA took part in the liberation of Toulon, the division's Chapius group based on the 7e Régiment Tirailleurs Algériens (7e RTA) headed for Marseille on August 20 along with armored columns of the 1ère DB, which had been screening the French advance toward the north and Aix-en-Provence. Marseille had some substantial hills shielding it on the landward side, rising up to 2,600ft. The French advance enjoyed almost complete freedom of movement as the concentration of German forces on the coast had left the major road network virtually unguarded except for military police units. This allowed de Lattre to deploy his forces on all sides of Marseille for the final attack, and to use the relatively open ground north of the city on either side of the Chaîne d'Etoile Mountains.

TOP
One of the bitterest skirmishes of the Toulon battle was the fight for Le Poudrière, a historic naval store built into four deep tunnels. The 3e RTA and M10 tank destroyers finally overcame it at dusk on August 22, a "Dantesque charnel-house" in the words of one French commander. (NARA)

BOTTOM
The French Army staged a tumultuous victory parade along Boulevard Strasbourg in Toulon on August 26 even though the Wehrmacht continued to cling to the Saint-Mandrier Peninsula overlooking the city. (NARA)

Marseille was held by 244. Infanterie-Division, which had already had one of its regiments transferred along with two regimental headquarters and two artillery batteries. The divisional commander, Generalleutnant Hans Schaefer, was appointed city commander for the defense. The garrison numbered about 13,000 including 2,500 Kriegsmarine and 3,900 Luftwaffe personnel. Schaefer was not convinced of the value of the numerous coastal defenses in the port or in the heavily fortified area of La Ciotat to the southeast, and so he ordered the Kreigsmarine to convert most of these troops into infantry and to deploy them in the second line of defense between Saint-Marcel and Saint-Jerome. By August 19, many of the defensive positions outside the city's defensive belt had been abandoned except for occasional patrols.

Besides the regular French forces involved in the fighting for Marseille, the FFI resistance played a much more significant role than in Toulon. In part this was owing to the enormous size of Marseille, France's second-largest city. The leadership of the FFI in Marseille had been decimated by Gestapo raids in July and the FFI combat units in the city were small, disorganized and poorly armed with probably no more than 500 armed insurgents. However, the frequent

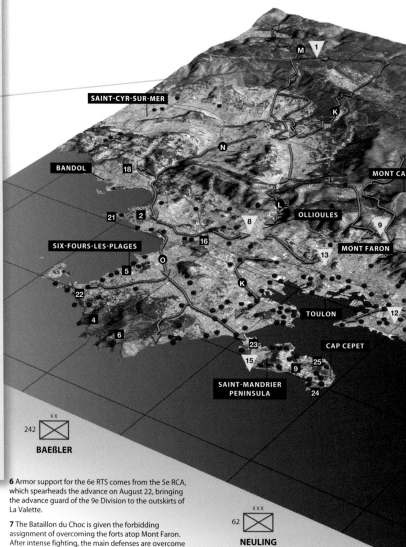

FRENCH UNITS

1ère Division de marche d'infanterie

A Bataillon de marche 1, 1ère Brigade d'infanterie
B Bataillon de marche 22, 1ère Brigade d'infanterie
C Bataillon de marche 4, 2e Brigade d'infanterie
D Bataillon de marche 5, 2e Brigade d'infanterie
E Bataillon de marche 21, 4e Brigade d'infanterie
F Bataillon de marche 24, 4e Brigade d'infanterie
G Bataillon d'infanterie de marine et du Pacifique, 4e Brigade d'infanterie

Attachments

H 5e compagnie, 18e Régiment de tirailleurs Sénégalais

3e Division d'infanterie Algeriénne

I 1er Bataillon, 3e Régiment de tirailleurs Algériens
J 3e Bataillon, 3e Régiment de tirailleurs Algériens
K 2e Bataillon, 4e Régiment de tirailleurs Tunisiens

Attachments

L 3e Régiment de spahis Algériens de reconnaissance
M 4e Escadron, 2e Régiment de spahis Algériens de reconnaissance
N 7e Régiment de chasseurs d'Afrique
O Régiment d'infanterie coloniale du Maroc (RICM)
P Battalion du Choc

9e Division d'infanterie coloniale

Q 2e Bataillon, 6e Régiment de tirailleurs Sénégalais
R 5e Compagnie, 6e Régiment de tirailleurs Sénégalais
S 6e Compagnie, 6e Régiment de tirailleurs Sénégalais
T 7e Compagnie, 6e Régiment de tirailleurs Sénégalais
U 3e Bataillon, 6e Régiment de tirailleurs Sénégalais

Attachments

V Groupe de commandos d'Afrique
W 5e Régiment de chasseurs d'Afrique

▼ EVENTS

1 Colonel Bonjour's 3e Spahis reach the road junction of Routes 2 and 8 on the afternoon of August 19, but find it defended by a strong roadblock. The advance guard is later reinforced by a squadron from the 2e Spahis and some armor, and pushes aside the roadblock the next day.

2 On August 19, two battalions of 3e RTA began advancing on Toulon by way of the desert plateau of Siou-Blanc, descending into the valleys north of the city on the morning of August 20.

3 The arrival of French infantry on the northern approaches of Toulon is obstructed by the formidable Mont Faron, as well as stubborn resistance by German troops in La Poudrière. The 3e DIA spends August 21 trying to clear German defenses in the area.

4 Colonel Salan's 6e RTS of the 9e DIC advances to the south to the road junction at Sollies-Pont that leads from the mountains into the shallow Gapeau River valley to the eastern outskirts of Toulon.

5 The 2e Brigade, 1ère DMI, is given the assignment of overcoming German defenses in Hyères, the headquarters of GR 918. The fiercest fighting centers around the Golf Hotel.

6 Armor support for the 6e RTS comes from the 5e RCA, which spearheads the advance on August 22, bringing the advance guard of the 9e Division to the outskirts of La Valette.

7 The Bataillon du Choc is given the forbidding assignment of overcoming the forts atop Mont Faron. After intense fighting, the main defenses are overcome by late afternoon.

8 The tanks of the 7e RCA reach the coast near Bandol on August 21, and then proceed toward the western suburbs of Toulon on August 22, awaiting the divisional reconnaissance of the 3e DIA, which reach the northern outskirts of Ollioules the next day.

9 By late on August 22, the infantry of the 3e RTA meets up with the Bataillon du Choc and begins moving into the city, heading for the main crossroads at Les Routes. The tunnels of La Poudrière are finally captured at dusk.

10 Although tanks of the 5e RCA had penetrated into La Vallette the day before, it takes the arrival of infantry from the 6e RTS to finally break the German grip on the town, finally allowing the 9e DIC to reach the outskirts of Toulon late August 23.

11 The Germans strongholds on the Giens Peninsula can only be reached by a narrow causeway, so late on August 23, the 5e Compagnie of the 18e RTS is ferried over to the southeastern end of the peninsula.

12 The 4e Brigade is the first element of the 1ère DMI to reach to outskirts of Toulon with troops of the 9e DIC pushing into the city further north.

13 The German garrison holding the Arsenal Maritime staged a desperate counterattack against the lead French elements in the western section of the city but is beaten back.

14 On August 24, de Lattre orders the 3e DIA to withdraw its forces from Toulon to reinforce the attack on neighboring Marseille. The brunt of the street fighting for Toulon is handed over to the 9e DIC and 1ère DMI. The port was finally reached on August 25, and defenses in the city largely collapse on August 26.

15 While the French staged a victory parade in Toulon on August 27, negotiations began with the last German hold-outs on the Saint-Mandrier Peninsula. At 0800hrs on August 28, the Saint-Mandrier strongpoints surrendered, completing the liberation of Toulon.

LIBERATION OF TOULON, AUGUST 19–28, 1944

Units from the French Armée B envelops and captures the city and its environs

GERMAN UNITS
62. Armee Korps
242. Infanterie Division
1   III/GR 917
2   1./GR 918
3   2./GR 918
4   3./GR 918
5   4./GR 918
6   5./GR 918
7   6./GR 918
8   7./GR 918
9   8./GR 918
10 12./GR 918
11 16./GR 918
12 18./GR 918
13 18 (Armen.)./GR 918
14 Feld-Ersatz-Bataillon 242
15 Pionier-Bataillon 242

16 II/AR 242 (12 x 100mm 100/19)
17 III/AR.242 (12 x 100mm 100/19)

244. Infanterie-Division
18 I/GR 934

Coastal defence batteries
19 1./MAA 627 (four x 138mm M10)
20 2./MAA 627 (four x 120mm M78)
21 1./le.MAA 682 (three x 138mm M10)
22 2./le.MAA 682 (three x 164mm M93-96)
23 3./le.MAA 682 (three x 100mm M97/17)
24 4./le.MAA 682 (four x 340mm M12)
25 5./le.MAA 682 (four x 164mm M/93-96)
26 6./le.MAA 682 (four x 75mm M08))
27 7./le.MAA 682 (four x 105mm M97)
28 HKAA 1191 (eight x 152mm, four x 100mm)
29 HKAA 1197 (12 x 149mm 149/19)

DIA

DE GOISLARD DE
MONSABERT

CUERS

SOLLIES-PONT

LLETTE-DU-VAR

LA CRAU

LA GARDE

HYÈRES

BROSSET
1 DMI

GIENS PENINSULA

AGNAN

Note: Gridlines are shown at intervals of 5km/3.10miles

65

TOP

The Toulon garrison made its last stand on the mountainous Saint-Mandrier Peninsula. Located on Cap Cepet at its eastern tip, the surviving gun turret of 4./leMAA 682 engaged in prolonged duels with Allied warships and was repeatedly bombed; one of its guns remained in operation until the end. The battery was based around a pair of cruiser turrets of the *Bretagne/Normandie* type installed by the French navy in 1928–35 and each armed with a pair of 340mm Mle 12 guns. (NARA)

BOTTOM

The arrival of the French Army in the Toulon area led to a popular uprising in Marseille. Here, a young FFI member takes shelter behind a signpost during the fighting there. (NARA)

Maquis operations had spooked the Germans badly and Gen.Lt. Schaefer thought that he might face as many as 80,000 insurgents. The FFI units provided an incendiary spark for an uprising, but the real trigger was the population at large, thoroughly fed up with the brutal German occupation, and inspired by the insurrection in Paris that had broken out on August 19. The Maquis threat was especially serious in the small towns outside Marseille where the FFI was most active. German attempts to set up combat outposts around the city were often frustrated by relentless FFI attacks.

French forces reached the outskirts of Marseille on August 21 near Auriol and de Lattre instructed Gén. Monsabert to begin the investment of the city with the three main units on hand, the 7e RTA, the 3e GTM (Groupes Tabors Marocains) and the armored units of Sudré's CC1 from the 1ère DB. The appearance of French troops in the suburbs led to the start of a disjointed popular insurrection and the establishment of a "provisional government"

within the city. In reality, the FFI hadn't the strength to wrest control of the city from the Germans, but the Germans did not have the strength to suppress the revolt.

German anti-tank positions in Aubagne on the main route into the city were simply avoided, and the French columns probed the outskirts of the city on August 22. Inside the city, the FFI attempted to seize the main post office without success. De Lattre recommended that Monsabert hold back until reinforcements arrived from the reduction of Toulon; de Lattre was also worried by American reports of the approach of the 11. Panzer-Division toward Aix-en-Provence. Nevertheless, Monsabert believed the German forces in the city were weak and disorganized, and he gave Colonel Abel Chappuis of the 7e RTA a free hand. This regiment advanced through most of the eastern suburbs against little opposition, and on the morning of August 23 they were coaxed into the heart of city to the acclaim of the growing French crowds.

The liberation of Marseille, August 20–27, 1944

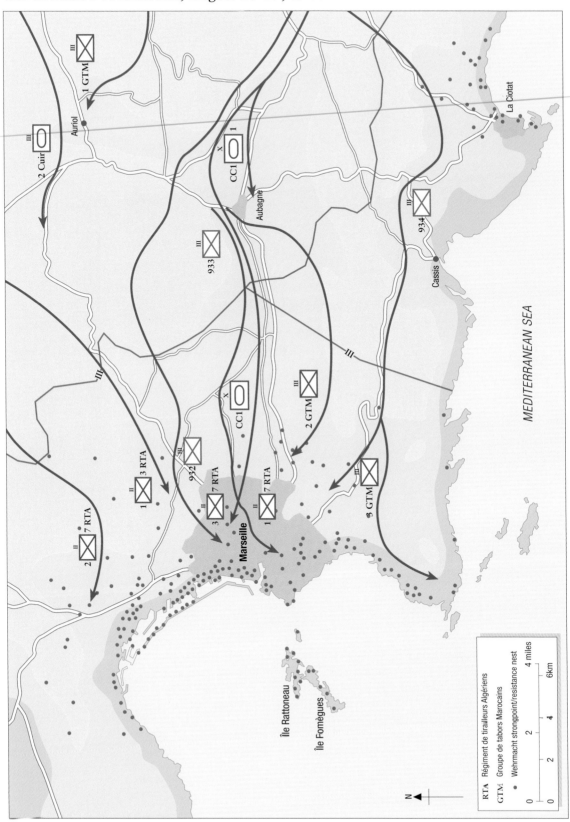

MEDITERRANEAN SEA

Auriol
La Ciotat
Aubagne
Cassis
Marseille
Île Rattoneau
Île Fomègues

1 GTM
2 Cuir
CC1 1
934
933
CC1
2 GTM
3 RTA
932
7 RTA
7 RTA
7 RTA
6 GTM
7 RTA

N

RTA   Régiment de tirailleurs Algériens
GTM   Groupe de tabors Marocains
•   Wehrmacht strongpoint/resistance nest

0   2   4   4 miles
0   2   4   6km

By the end of the day, the 7e RTA had reached the waterfront. The 3e DIA attempted to negotiate a capitulation of the German garrison with the aid of the German consul general but could not come to an agreement and the truce expired at 1900hrs. The fighting for the city took three days. The Vieux Port (old port) fell almost immediately and large sections of the city came under French control. The German garrison remained ensconced in the numerous fortifications along the seacoast as well as in the heights near Notre-Dame-de-la-Garde. On August 25, much of the remainder of the 3e DIA that had been fighting in Toulon arrived in the southeastern region of Marseille and overwhelmed the last hold-outs in the southern sector.

TOP
A pair of B-25 Mitchell bombers of the 488th Bomb Squadron are seen over Marseille during a strike mission to eliminate German coastal gun batteries during the fight for the port. (NARA)

BOTTOM
Algerian troops of Chappuis' 7e RTA cautiously advance up a street in the foothills below the Notre-Dame-de-la-Garde basilica on August 28. (NARA)

Allied air attack and warships pummeled German coastal artillery positions on the Île Ratonneau and Île Pomegues off the coast. On August 26, French infantry backed by tanks finally overcame the heights of Notre-Dame-de-la-Garde and the defenders surrendered around 1000hrs. The strongholds around Fort Saint-Nicholas on the waterfront capitulated on August 27 after having been subjected to point-blank fire from French field artillery. By now, the French actions were mostly mop-up operations of the numerous small German strongpoints scattered around the city and in its suburbs. French casualties were 1,825 men killed and wounded and about 11,000 German troops surrendered. The capture of Marseille was a month earlier than expected in Allied planning, on D+13 instead of D+45. As at Toulon, German engineer

TOP
The Notre-Dame-de-la-Garde basilica comes under German artillery firing during the fighting for Marseille. The church was the source of some controversy as the Wehrmacht intentionally did not occupy it during the fighting, but the French FFI used it as a base of operations against nearby German positions. (NARA)

BOTTOM
A French sailor inspects an abandoned German 75mm Pak 97/38 anti-tank gun that had been covering one of the boulevards in the center of the city. (NARA)

The Kriegsmarine attempted to deny the port facilities to the Allies by extensive demolishing of key facilities and scuttling of ships. The transport *Cap Corse* was sunk in the narrow channel between Fort Saint-Nicholas and Fort Saint-Jean, blocking access to the Vieux Port. (NARA)

teams had done a thorough job destroying facilities, and obstructing the harbor with sunken ships and mines. Owing to the port's importance, specialized US forces moved into the port immediately to begin its rehabilitation. The first Liberty ship unloaded a cargo on shore on September 15, and by the end of the month the port had already handled over 100,000 tons of cargo. Marseille became the main Allied port in southern France and by October, the southern France ports accounted for over 500,000 tons of cargo each month. In total, Marseille and the other southern ports accounted for nearly a third of the Allied cargo delivered to the ETO in 1944 and 1945.

THE MONTÉLIMAR BATTLE SQUARE

The Wehrmacht planned to withdraw Korps Kneiss up the eastern bank of the Rhône, while the 4.Luftwaffe Feldkorps, which had been stationed further west near the Spanish frontier, would retreat up the west bank of the Rhône. On August 21, 11. Panzer-Division sent another small *Kampfgruppe* with about ten tanks toward Aix-en-Provence to discourage any further advance by the US 3rd Division, which was moving on Aix with the aim of following the retreating German forces up the Rhône Valley.

The unexpected evacuation of 157. Reserve-Division east into the Alps allowed TF Butler to advance rapidly in parallel to the German line of retreat, some 45 miles further east. The senior American commanders began to realize that they could strike at the flank of the retreating German columns rather than simply chase them from behind with the 3rd Infantry Division. Instead of continuing to push US units into the vacuum around Grenoble, they decided on a bolder course: to re-direct TF Butler to the Rhône in an effort to cut off the path of the German retreat around Montélimar followed by the 36th Division. This was an extremely risky gambit, as TF Butler and the 36th Division would be confronting forces many times their size, connected along a distant, narrow and convoluted logistic link back to the beachhead

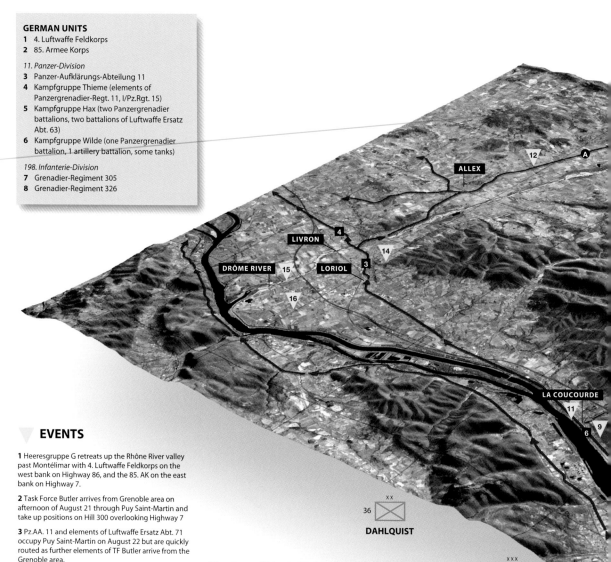

EVENTS

1 Heeresgruppe G retreats up the Rhône River valley past Montélimar with 4. Luftwaffe Feldkorps on the west bank on Highway 86, and the 85. AK on the east bank on Highway 7.

2 Task Force Butler arrives from Grenoble area on afternoon of August 21 through Puy Saint-Martin and take up positions on Hill 300 overlooking Highway 7

3 Pz.AA. 11 and elements of Luftwaffe Ersatz Abt. 71 occupy Puy Saint-Martin on August 22 but are quickly routed as further elements of TF Butler arrive from the Grenoble area.

4 Elements of the 141st Infantry continue to arrive, followed by the 142nd Infantry. Dahlquist sets up a defensive perimeter along the Roubion River.

5 Around dawn on August 23, Pz.AA. 11 pushes into Sauzet but is quickly pushed out by the 141st Infantry. A US infantry battalion heads out of Sauzet around 1630hrs to try to capture Montélimar but is thrown back by a determined German defense.

6 Another attack by the 141st Infantry on Montélimar on August 24 is rebuffed, and a German counterattack clears most of Hill 300 and parts of Hill 430.

7 Kampfgruppe Thieme pushes through a few roadblocks of the 117th Cavalry Squadron around noon on August 25 at the start of a planned offensive. The German forces reach Crest and push southward but are stopped by elements of TF Butler. An attack by Pz.AA 11 toward Puy Saint-Martin fails to materialize.

8 Kampfgruppe Hax starts its attack on August 25 only at 1400hrs trying to secure Hill 300 and the western side of Hill 430, but fails to advance. Likewise, an attack in the same area by GR 305 fails.

9 Kampfgruppe Wilde sets off on its August 25 attack late at around 1500hrs, intending to push US forces out of La Coucourde but fails to make any inroads. The attack on Hill 430 is repeated on August 26 with meager results.

10 An attack by GR 326 overwhelms a company from the 111th Engineers, but is beaten back by artillery. An attack on August 26 pushes into the gap between 141st and 142nd infantry near Bonlieu but fails to take purchase.

11 Task Force Butler pushes out of La Coucourde and sets up roadblocks on Highway 7. In desperation, Wietersheim personally leads a scratch force of tanks and Panzergrenadiers late that day which manages to clear the highway for the time being.

12 Pz.AA. 11 again tries to push down Highway 86C and reaches within two miles of Crest before being stopped by elements of TF Butler.

13 The German attacks of August 25–26 force Truscott to send reinforcements, two battalions of the 157th Infantry, which begin moving into the northern sector of the Montélimar battle square on August 26.

14 From August 27, the focus of the fighting shifts to Loriol as 85. AK tries to withdraw its last forces over the Drôme River. Besides the newly arrived 157th Infantry, Dahlquist begins shifting infantry and artillery battalions from the Roubion River line up to the east of Loriol.

15 Although the Drôme River bridge south of Loriol was dropped by US artillery and air strikes on August 25, the Wehrmacht establishes fords, ferries and pontoon bridges The 36th Division tries to interdict the crossing with artillery.

16 By August 29, 85. AK has mostly passed over the Drôme with the 142nd Infantry in pursuit; the 157th Infantry mops up Highway 7 and the Drôme River crossings.

THE MONTÉLIMAR BATTLE SQUARE: AUGUST 23–26, 1944
US VI Corps interdicts the German the retreat along the Rhône Valley

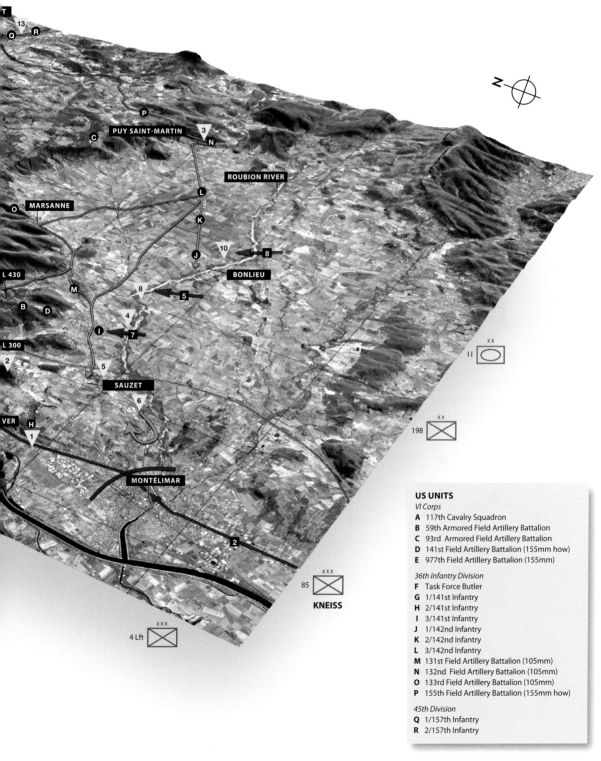

T
13
Q R

P
PUY SAINT-MARTIN   3
C   N

ROUBION RIVER

L
MARSANNE
O   K

10   8
J
BONLIEU
L 430
M   8
B   D   5
L 300   I   7
2
5
SAUZET
6
VER H
1

MONTÉLIMAR
2

II   xx

198   xx

85   xxx

KNEISS

4 Lft   xxx

US UNITS

VI Corps
A 117th Cavalry Squadron
B 59th Armored Field Artillery Battalion
C 93rd Armored Field Artillery Battalion
D 141st Field Artillery Battalion (155mm how)
E 977th Field Artillery Battalion (155mm)

36th Infantry Division
F Task Force Butler
G 1/141st Infantry
H 2/141st Infantry
I 3/141st Infantry
J 1/142nd Infantry
K 2/142nd Infantry
L 3/142nd Infantry
M 131st Field Artillery Battalion (105mm)
N 132nd Field Artillery Battalion (105mm)
O 133rd Field Artillery Battalion (105mm)
P 155th Field Artillery Battalion (155mm how)

45th Division
Q 1/157th Infantry
R 2/157th Infantry

73

RIGHT
Graveyard of Heeresgruppe G. Route 7 on either side of Montélimar was littered with the debris of retreating German columns, pummeled from the air by Allied air power and artillery. (NARA)

BOTTOM
The remains of a German column burned out on the southern approaches of Montélimar. The German infantry units were poorly equipped with motor transport and many of the vehicles destroyed during the fighting were civilian French vehicles impressed into service during the desperate retreat. (NARA)

over poor mountain roads. By this stage, the main logistical problem facing the US Army was the lack of fuel. The three divisions of Truscott's VI Corps consumed about 100,000 gallons of fuel per day, but the reserves totaled only 11,000 gallons on the beachhead supplemented by captured stocks of about 26,000 gallons. Allied planning had not anticipated the rapidity of the Allied advance and the continuing fuel shortages would slow US operations around Montélimar.

An M8 75mm howitzer motor carriage passes by a burned-out German column on the outskirts of Montélimar. (NARA)

Task Force Butler began moving west toward the Rhône River on August 21, with an advance party from the 753rd Tank Battalion taking up positions on Hill 300 which ran parallel to Route 7 about five miles north of Montélimar. Once overlooking Route 7, this spearhead began firing on the retreating German columns. Butler's forces totaled only a few hundred troops and a few dozen armored vehicles yet were standing aside a flowing stream of thousands of German troops and hundreds of vehicles. Task Force Butler was too weak and too scattered to attack and hold Montélimar until more ammunition and reinforcements from the 36th Division arrived.

Wiese of AOK 19 was shocked by the sudden appearance of a threat on his flank. Quickly realizing that TF Butler posed a greater challenge than the 3rd Division behind his forces, he ordered Wietersheim to reorient 11. Panzer-Division northward to deal with the flank threat, and substituted Pioneer Bataillon 668 as the rearguard. The first unit to arrive around Montélimar was the division's reconnaissance battalion, Panzer-Aufklärungs-Abteilung 11 (PzAA 11). Reinforced by troops from a Luftwaffe infantry training regiment, a hasty attack toward the road junction at Puy cut off TF Butler, but this was short lived when the German force was pushed aside as further units from TF Butler began to arrive from further east near Gap. Nevertheless, this attack made it clear that the American position astride Route 7 was very precarious until more substantial forces arrived.

Dahlquist was slowly moving the 36th Division toward Montélimar, having to substitute elements of the 45th Division for his own battalions in the Grenoble area before heading westward. Truscott continued to prod him on August 22, reaffirming that Montélimar, and not Grenoble was his focus.

MONTÉLIMAR'S DEADLY CORRIDOR (pp. 76–77)

Route 7 running through Montélimar to Lyon became a corridor of death for AOK 19 with hundreds of burned-out vehicles lining the path northward. The retreating German units were hounded by the US Army's 3rd Division approaching from Avignon to the south, strafed by Hellcats and Spitfires from Allied carriers off shore, and harassed by artillery from the 36th Division menacingly lurking in the hills to the east.

The retreating columns were doggedly defended by 11. Panzer-Division, and especially by its fleet mobile force, Panzer-Aufklärungs-Abteilung 11. This was its divisional reconnaissance element, and the first to arrive in the Montélimar area on August 21. Joined by elements of Luftwaffe-Ersatz-Abt. 71, the regiment gained control of the road junction of Puy-Saint-Martin on August 22, temporarily cutting off TF Butler, which was the first US unit to threaten Route 7. However, the German *Kampfgruppe* was chased out of Puy that day as further elements of TF Butler arrived from the Grenoble area.

Here we see a column from Pz.Aufk.Abt. 11 as it attempts to move past retreating German columns on Route 7. Most of the units of AOK 19 lacked any organic transport and so relied on confiscated French commercial and civilian vehicles for their trek to the German border. Municipal buses were a prize catch, and many fell victim to marauding Allied fighters as can be seen to the right **(1)**. The forlorn attempts to camouflage the vehicles

with tree branches **(2)** were undermined by lack of cover along the Rhône River valley, especially the highway itself.

The lead vehicles of the Pz.Aufk.Abt. 11 patrol are the stubby little SdKfz 250/8 **(3)**, which was an assault gun version of the normal leichter Schützenpanzerwagen SdKfz 250 half-track, the workhorse of German armored reconnaissance units. The basic version carried a scout section, but it was configured in a myriad of specialized versions including radio-command, mortar and heavy weapons carriers. The SdKfz 250/8 version was armed with a short Kwk 37 75mm gun, and these were issued to the fourth platoon in each company to provide fire support.

Pz.Aufk.Abt. 11 spent most of the last week of August 1944 in the northern sector of the Montélimar "battle square" alongside Kampfgruppe Thieme, harassing the US 36th Division's supply line along the Loriol–Grane highway. It frequently skirmished with its American counterpart, the 117th Cavalry Reconnaissance Squadron (Mechanized), which was attempting to keep open the logistics lines back toward Grenoble. They would again face each other in one of the most bitter battles of the campaign on September 2–3 in Montreval where a spearhead of the 117th CRSM attempted to cut off the retreating German columns, only to be encircled and crushed by Pz.Aufk.Abt. 11 supported by the divisional engineer battalion.

The three battalions of the 141st Infantry were the first to arrive and took up positions on Hill 300 and the surrounding hills north of Montélimar. As more units arrived, Dahlquist gradually built up a defensive perimeter along the Roubion River with the 142nd Infantry. Like many Italian front veterans, the 36th Division was very wary of bold actions against the Germans until a bare minimum of defensive precautions had been taken. Dahlquist wanted to establish a viable defensive perimeter away from Route 7 to shield the vital road network behind his forces. This slowed the American advance against Route 7 and limited the forces trying to block the road. A more typical American tactic would have been to interdict the road using artillery, but the lack of fuel and trucks to transport the artillery ammunition left Dahlquist's force chronically short throughout the fight for the Montélimar "Battle Square," with barely enough to provide defensive coverage.

The slow pace of Dahlquist's advance was mirrored on the German side, with Wietersheim having a hard time getting his forces over to the east bank of the Rhône, and then moving them northward to Montélimar amidst the traffic jams of retreating German columns. Kampfgruppe Thieme with a battalion of Panzergrenadiers, ten tanks and a self-propelled artillery battery finally arrived around noon on August 23, but the remainder of the division didn't reach Montélimar until August 24.

Dahlquist tried to push the 2/141st Infantry into Montélimar on August 24 but Wietersheim counterattacked and cleared the ridge of Hill 300. The growing intensity of German counterattacks reaffirmed Dahlquist's insistence on reinforcing his defenses along the Roubion River line before embarking on Truscott's mission of interdicting the German traffic up Route 7. To make

An M10 3in. GMC of the 601st Tank Destroyer Battalion passes through Montélimar on August 30 along with other elements of the 3rd Division that had been hounding the German retreat. The town is littered with burned-out German trucks, dead horses and other war debris. (NARA)

In the wake of the fighting, a wrecker truck of the 734th Ordnance Battalion recovers a PzKpfw III tank from the fields north of Crest. Over a dozen of these obsolete tanks were in use by 11. Panzer-Division as command and forward observer vehicles in the headquarters company and artillery battalion. Kampfgruppe Thiele used some in their skirmishes with the 117th Cavalry in the northern sector of the Montélimar "battle square." (NARA)

matters worse, on the evening of August 24, the Germans captured a copy of Dahlquist's operational plans for August 25, describing his forces in detail. Wiese formed a provisional corps under Wietersheim to counterattack and overwhelm the menace on his flank once and for all. The improvised corps included 11. Panzer-Division, 198. Infanterie-Division, a Luftwaffe infantry training regiment, a flak regiment and a railroad artillery battalion with five heavy-caliber railway guns, and it outnumbered Dahlquist's force more than three to one. Wiese intended to smash the two regiments of the 36th Division so thoroughly that Route 7 would remain clear of American threats long enough to get the rest of Korps Kneiss through; the bulk of these units were still 35 miles south of Montélimar.

The attack on August 25 was a flop. Kampfgruppe Thieme in the north on the Drôme River pushed through a weak American cavalry screening force down the road toward Allex and Grane, threatening the 36th Division supply lines, but this was the only success of the day. The other five *Kampfgruppen* along the Roubion River started their assault much later than intended with very little coordination owing to the chaos around Montélimar and they were beaten back by US infantry and potent artillery in the hills above. The 2/143rd Infantry counterattacked and regained control of Hill 300 while the 1/141st Infantry supported by four tanks and seven M10 tank destroyers managed to cut Route 7 at La Coucourde. In frustration over the dismal results of the day's attack, Wietersheim himself gathered up a scratch force after dark and assaulted the American roadblock at La Coucourde, reopening the highway after midnight.

The push by Kampfgruppe Thieme around Grane concerned Truscott enough that he ordered 45th Division to deploy the 157th Infantry and the 191st Tank Battalion into the northern area of the Montélimar "battle square." Unhappy over the poor results of the August 25 attack, Wiese dissolved the temporary corps and put most of its forces under Kneiss who was instructed to continue attacks to clear the Montélimar sector. The fighting on August 26 and 27 was largely a stalemate with the German forces unable to overcome the American defenses, while at the same time the 36th Division was unable to establish blocking positions across Route 7. As this fighting was going on, 4. Luftwaffe Feldkorps passed Montélimar on the west bank of the Rhône on August 26, largely undisturbed except by air attack. At dusk on August 27, Wiese ordered Kneiss to pull the remaining forces north on August 28, with 198. Infanterie-Division to remain as a rearguard and escape as best it could. Kneiss tried to extract the remainder of his forces on the night of August 28/29, but two columns of the rearguard 198. Infanterie-Division ran into a pre-dawn advance of the 143rd Infantry toward Montélimar and suffered heavy losses. Montélimar was sandwiched between the 15th Infantry, 3rd Division, advancing from the south and the 141st Infantry from the north and finally fell on the morning of August 29 with Gen. Richter of 198. Infanterie-Division becoming one of the prisoners. During the mopping-up operations around Montélimar about 3,500 German troops were captured.

With Montélimar cleared, the fighting shifted to the northern sector around the Drôme River crossings and GR 757 was decimated trying to keep the crossings open. The 142nd Infantry did not finally clear the northern side of the Drôme until August 31, finally ending the battle for the Montélimar "battle square." AOK 19 suffered about 2,100 combat casualties during the Montélimar fighting and a further 8,000 captured on either side of the Rhône; American casualties totaled about 1,575.

The fighting for Montélimar was a disappointment for both sides. Truscott had hoped to disrupt the German retreat severely. But the focus of Allied actions in the last week of August was the liberation of the ports; Truscott did not have the forces or the fuel more seriously to contest the German withdrawal. The 36th Division might have been able to interdict Route 7 by artillery fire, but the field artillery under their control was continuously short of ammunition. Underlying Truscott's problems was the pessimistic planning behind Operation *Dragoon*, which did not consider the probability of a German withdrawal and so did not include enough mechanized forces or fuel. The Seventh Army was a victim of its own success; the landings and subsequent expansion of the bridgehead had gone so quickly that when it was handed a rare tactical opportunity it could not fully exploit it. Blaskowitz and Wiese were relieved that they had not suffered more catastrophic losses, but the quick collapse of the port defenses and the costly withdrawal effort were evidence of profound demoralization in the Wehrmacht in southern France.

THE RACE TO DIJON

Patch's Seventh Army had a good appreciation of German intentions thanks to Ultra communication decrypts, and an OKW signal from August 25, received on August 28, laid out the German intentions to regroup around Dijon and to use 11. Panzer-Division to prevent a repeat of the Montélimar mess by shielding the retreating forces on the east side of the Rhône. Patch maintained the original plans to use Truscott's VI Corps as the main pursuit force heading up Route 7 to Lyon and beyond, with French forces providing a covering force to the west. Since it would take de Lattre some time to secure Toulon, Marseille and the surrounding coastal area, only a part of these forces were available for the pursuit to Lyon. The French II Corps provided two divisions to cover the west bank of the Rhône, with du Vigier's 1ère DB at the extreme left, and Brosset's 1ère DMI on the west bank of the Rhône. Patch hoped that if the 3rd and 45th divisions could move fast enough, they could reach Bourg and block the main German escape route.

CHAMPAGNE AND DESPERATION (pp. 82–83)

While most of Truscott's VI Corps moved west to chase the Germans up the Rhône Valley, the US paratroopers of the 1st Airborne Task Force and the 1st Special Services Force were sent east to speed the Germans' withdrawal into Italy. The operation was later dubbed the "Champagne Campaign" as the paratroopers and Special Forces units liberated the seaside resorts of the Riviera and slopes of the French Alps. The US special operations units were very lightly equipped, so Rear Admiral Morton Deyo's Right Flank Force was assigned to provide them with fire support from the sea.

With the Kriegsmarine powerless to contest the Allied naval forces, in late August the K-Verbände (Kleinkampfverbände: small combat teams) were ordered to deploy their mini-sub and assault boat units to the Franco-Italian border to contest the Allied fleet. The first to arrive was 1./K-Flotilla 364 commanded by Oberleutnant zur See Peter Berger. This unit was equipped with the Marder mini-sub, an evolution of the earlier Neger human torpedo first used off Anzio in February 1944. The Marder was constructed from two torpedoes stacked one atop the other; the upper torpedo had the warhead removed and a small steering compartment added in its place, with seating for a single pilot. The Marder cruised to its target near the surface using the propulsion of the upper torpedo, with only a small plexiglass dome exposed to allow the pilot to steer.

Berger's unit arrived at their staging base at Menton, east of Monte Carlo, and their 12 Marder submarines were hurriedly prepared for action. The dozen Marders set out from Menton at 0600hrs on September 5 heading toward the US Navy warships off the coast. The US Navy ships had been warned

about the threat of midget subs, quite possibly from Ultra signals intelligence. The Marders first passed through a screen of minesweepers, and USS Incredible (AM-249) claimed to hit at least two of them with gunfire. The French destroyer leader Le Malin spotted the submerged flotilla inbound around 0812hrs and alerted the neighboring USS Ludlow (DD-483) **(1)**, which was shelling landward targets. Ludlow opened fire on the nearest Marder **(2)** as seen here using its 20mm anti-aircraft cannon **(3)** and then steered towards the incoming German flotilla, dropping depth charges. The first attack sank one Marder, and the pilot bobbed to the surface where he was later captured. A hunt began with Le Malin engaging one with gunfire and Ludlow sinking two more with gunfire and depth charges. Even though only the little dome of the Marder was visible, its round shape glinted in the sunlight, exposing the Marder to attack. Of the five Marders that actually reached the Allied ships, only one returned and four were lost.

This was only the beginning of a futile campaign by German and Italian naval commandos to attack the Allied fleet on the Riviera through the rest of September. The next major attack on September 9 involved 14 Marders, three German and three Italian assault boats. The assault boats were small craft loaded with explosives that were either radio-controlled, or steered to the target by crews who dove overboard at the last minute. Two US destroyers and a PT boat were credited with sinking ten of them in the ensuing massacre. The attacks petered out in late September, though German naval commando attacks continued into 1945 with little to show for their desperate heroism.

TOP
Following the liberation of the ports, the French divisions began pushing up Route 7 toward Lyon. This is Belfort, an M8 75mm assault gun of the 1ère Division blindée, moving through Avignon on August 30 with a column of FFI alongside.

BOTTOM
Although Lyon had largely been abandoned by the Wehrmacht when entered by French units on September 3, sniping continued from rearguards and members of the collaborationist French Milice. Here, a mixture of troops and FFI members exchange shots with snipers in the Hôtel Dieu hospital across the river. (NARA)

Blaskowitz's main concern was to push his units into and through Lyon as rapidly as possible as there were reports that an insurrection had broken out in the city. The 4. Luftwaffe Feldkorps, which had escaped largely unscathed up the west side of the Rhône, was assigned to regain control of the city and hold it open through the night of August 31 by which time he expected that his forces would have passed through. Blaskowitz instructed 11. Panzer-Division to destroy all the bridges over the Rhône and Ain rivers east of Lyon in hopes of thwarting any American drive toward Bourg.

The race between the 11. Panzer-Division and the 45th Division was won by the Americans, who passed over both rivers and reached the area north of Meximieux by September 1. Over the next few days, there were several sharp skirmishes between both units which tied down the 45th Division's advance.

The race to Lyon, August 29–September 3, 1944

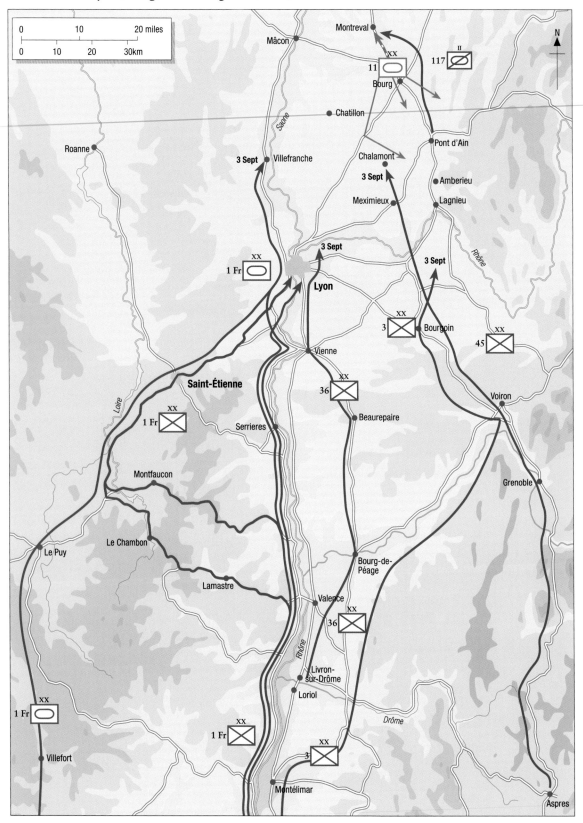

A *Kampfgruppe* from 11. Panzer-Division launched an attack into Meximieux behind the 45th Division's main force, colliding with two reserve companies of the 179th Infantry and the regimental headquarters. The *Kampfgruppe* reported that it had destroyed the regiment when in fact US casualties were about 215 men, two M10 tank destroyers, two M8 armored cars and a few vehicles, while the Germans lost 85 men killed, 41 captured, 12 tanks, three self-propelled guns and several vehicles.

Lyon was enveloped by September 2 and Patch gave the French divisions the honor of liberating the city; by September 3 most of the German forces had already escaped. Efforts to cut off the escape route further north at Bourg were frustrated by German defenses. Truscott used his sole mobile force, the overworked 117th Cavalry Reconnaissance Squadron, to try an end-run around Bourg by taking the towns of Montreval and Marboz further north. This squadron pushed into Montreval on September 3 after a first attempt the night before had failed. Two troops from the cavalry squadron routed a force of about 300 German rear service personnel but quickly found themselves trapped by an 11. Panzer-Division *Kampfgruppe* based around the division's reconnaissance battalion reinforced with tanks, assault guns and engineers. During the one-sided skirmish that ensued, the 117th CRSM had five men killed and 126 taken prisoner along with 20 jeeps, 15 M8 armored cars and two M5A1 light tanks destroyed. By this stage, most of AOK 19's forces had escaped by an alternate route through Mâcon. The only German force to fall victim to the Allied advance was the rearguard of 4. Luftwaffe Feldkorps, which lost 2,000 troops, captured by CC Kientz of the 1ère DB.

The first two weeks of September saw a continued pursuit of the ragtag Heeresgruppe G through central France, with Blaskowitz unable to hold any of the intended objectives such as Dijon or Besançon. Patch's Seventh Army was equally frustrated in its attempts to outrace and trap any significant

The 11. Panzer-Division attempted to brush back the pursuing US 45th Division, staging a counterattack into the streets of Meximieux in the first days of September. This Panther is one of nine Panzers lost in the street fighting. (NARA)

portion of the German force owing to overextension and the lingering gas problem. By September 10, patrols from the *Dragoon* units began meeting up with forward patrols from Patton's Third Army. In the process, they trapped the final AOK 1 column under Gen. Elster from the Bordeaux area on the Loire River, and 20,000 troops surrendered on September 15.

Patch had hoped to seize the Belfort Gap, but on September 14, the chase largely came to an end. That day, the Allied command structure transitioned from the Mediterranean command structure to the European chain of command. Jacob Devers took charge of the 6th Army Group, which reported to Eisenhower and SHAEF, not Wilson and AFHQ. Patch remained in command of the US Seventh Army, but the French units that had reported to him now reported to de Lattre's 1ère Armée Française. Eisenhower was not overly concerned about the Belfort Gap, and the forces in the ETO were running out of fuel and supplies after a victorious but exhausting summer campaign. The race northward came to a halt in the foothills of the Vosges Mountains. The Seventh Army had finally run out of steam after a wildly successful month-long campaign.

Heeresgruppe G was an emaciated shadow of the force that had existed a month earlier, having lost more than half its forces. As of the evening of September 14, Heeresgruppe G had suffered 143,250 casualties of which about 7,000 had been killed, 20,000 wounded, and 105,000 captured and these totals did not include the nominally operational formations left behind in the Atlantic *Festung* ports, which added more than 25,000 troops to the tally of losses. Not surprisingly, its combat units were a shambles with most of its infantry divisions down to 3,000 men or less. The 11. Panzer-Division was the only formation to emerge relatively intact with about 6,500 men, but it had barely a dozen tanks and two assault guns in service. Allied casualties were substantially less with the US VI Corps having 4,500 battle casualties and the French Armée B slightly higher numbers depending on whether or not FFI units are tallied. Both sides faced a grueling autumn campaign in the hard terrain of the Vosges Mountains.

AFTERMATH

Operation *Dragoon* was one of the most remarkable victories of the Allied forces in the summer of 1944, liberating nearly two-thirds of France in a lightning one-month campaign. Allied planning had not anticipated such a rapid advance; the original plans did not expect Seventh Army to reach the Rhône Valley until mid-October and Lyon until mid-November. Undoubtedly, the diversion of Wehrmacht strength from southern France to Normandy in July 1944 fatally weakened any potential defense. The credit for the operation largely falls to Gen. George C. Marshall and the planners in Washington, who had steadfastly pushed for such an operation in spite of Churchill's adamant preference for continued peripheral operations in Italy and elsewhere in the Mediterranean. The speed of the advance can also be credited in part to the exceptional role of the FFI in this theater. While the Maquis was seldom strong enough to overcome the Wehrmacht in a deliberate battle, the Wehrmacht occupation units were so intimidated by the Maquis threat that they were

A scene repeated many times in Provence in the summer of 1944. An isolated German soldier hunted down by some young maquisards and brought to a US Army post. (NARA)

TOP

The junction of Patton's Third Army and Patch's Seventh Army around Dijon in mid-September trapped the more distant German columns. On September 15, Gen.Maj. Botho Elster and his staff negotiated the surrender of the 20,000 troops in their column from AOK 1 in a pocket near Romorantin on the Loire River with US officers. Elster had previously been a military governor of the Biarritz area on the Atlantic coast and was ordered by Berlin to head the withdrawal effort from Biarritz and Bordeaux. (NARA)

BOTTOM

The conclusion of the *Dragoon* operation in mid-September led to a major reorganization of Allied forces in central France, with Lt. Gen. Jacob Devers taking over command of the new 6th Army Group consisting of Patch's US Seventh Army and de Lattre's 1ère Armée Française. These forces were resubordinated from Wilson's Mediterranean command to Eisenhower's European command. Here on October 23, 1944, Devers is seen decorating de Lattre with the Legion of Merit—Commander's Degree for his leadership in the capture of Toulon and Marseille. (NARA)

unwilling and unable to set up blocking positions on the approaches to Grenoble even though the terrain favored the defense. As a result, small US formations were able to advance against Grenoble with hardly any opposition. This sudden drive north positioned the Seventh Army to strike Heeresgruppe G's Rhône withdrawal route from an unexpected direction, causing a chaotic and hasty retreat. The campaign might have taken a very different course were it not for the unanticipated flank attack against Montélimar.

The expeditious liberation of southern and central France greatly simplified Allied planning for operations against Germany in 1944–45. A counter-factual argument can be made to explain the value of Operation *Dragoon* to later

Allied operations against Germany. Had Patch's Seventh Army remained in the Italian theater and Heeresgruppe G left in place, the Allied lodgement area north of the Loire River would have been subjected to flank attack through the autumn of 1944 by units of Heeresgruppe G, reinforced from Germany via Alsace. A "Battle of the Bulge" counteroffensive would have occurred sooner and in a different direction if the Wehrmacht had not been pushed out of central France by Operation *Dragoon*. Hitler had already planned such an offensive for September 1944 to cut off Patton's Third Army, but this was reduced in scale when Dijon fell so rapidly and the counteroffensive degenerated into a series of poorly executed attacks in Lorraine. Even if a major German autumn counteroffensive had not succeeded, it would have delayed the Allied advance into Germany and forced the Allies to extend their forces to defend the lodgement area, or to conduct a campaign to liberate central and southern France from northern France. To extend the argument further, the addition of Seventh Army to the Italian theater might have resulted in a successful Po Valley campaign in the autumn of 1944 via a landing on the gulf of Genoa instead of the actual spring offensive of 1945 through the Gothic line. But in spite of Churchill's fantasies, an Allied thrust into southern Germany or Austria from the Italian side of the Brenner Pass was preposterous given the difficulties of the Alpine terrain and the Wehrmacht's diehard defense of German soil in 1944–45. The "soft underbelly of Europe" was anything but soft as witnessed by the weary veterans of the Monte Cassino, Salerno, Anzio and Gothic Line campaigns.

THE BATTLEFIELDS TODAY

Mount Faron on the approaches of Toulon viewed from the Royal Tower to the southeast. The Germans used this tower as a flak position in 1944. (Robert Forczyk)

The sun, sand, and surf of the Provence coast has made it one of France's principal tourist destinations. The brief fighting along the coast has left few memories and few traces. For history buffs, Operation *Dragoon* is overshadowed by the Roman ruins and scenic Vauban forts. Fort Faron in the scenic hills above Toulon has a museum devoted to the campaign. Some German coastal bunkers still stubbornly resist the encroachments of man and nature but they are hard to find without a specialist guide. The sunken LST-282 has become a curiosity for sport divers with a small memorial nearby. There are numerous small monuments and memorials scattered along the coast, but certainly not on the scale seen in Normandy. The devastation along the Montélimar corridor has long since disappeared. One of the few guides to the battlefield today is *After the Battle* magazine's No. 110 (2000) issue devoted to this subject which shows some of the best known images of the campaign and ties them to their current location.

FURTHER READING

Operation *Dragoon* remains obscure more from lack of attention than lack of good published histories. In the US, a large fraction of World War II history books are British books republished under American imprints. Since British historians have generally ignored this subject owing to the relatively modest British role, this has tended to diminish coverage. Few French military histories are translated and printed in the US or Britain, so the extensive French literature on this subject is largely unknown amongst the English-reading public.

The official US Army history was the last of the World War II "Green Book" campaign histories to appear, published only in 1991. However, it benefited from the delay since it was able to incorporate recently declassified material, such as Ultra intelligence, which is essential to understanding US decision-making in the days after the landing. Nevertheless, the multi-volume Seventh Army study remains a very useful account, and provides more detail than the later army study. Paul Gaujac is the French historian most intimately connected with the history of the Provence campaign and he has published several excellent monographs over the past decade. The French role in Operation *Dragoon* is well covered in both French and English. The Funk book provides an excellent study of the interplay between Allied special operations and the Maquis. Although the German side lacks a comprehensive history, there is an ample selection of reports by former German commanders for the Foreign Military Studies program of the US Army Office of Military History immediately after the war; I used the set at the US Army Military History Institute at Carlisle Barracks, Pennsylvania. The naval side of the landings is also well covered from both the US and British sides. The air campaign has not yet been the subject of a dedicated monograph, although the Craven and Cate history details the USAAF. I used a number of archival sources to cover gaps in the published sources, including Seventh Army records at the US National Archives and Records Administration (NARA) at College Park. I also used the NARA collection of captured German records where available; the AOK 19 files have extensive detail on the fortification efforts in late 1943.

Official studies
Airborne Missions in the Mediterranean 1942–1945 (USAF Historical Division: 1955)
Invasion Europe: Invasion of the South of France (HMSO: 1994)
Le 2e CA dans la Bataille pour la Libération de la France: Rapports d'Opérations
      (French Army: 1947)
The Seventh United States Army in France and Germany 1944–45, Volume 1
      (US Army: 1946)

US Army Foreign Military Studies
Blaskowitz, Johannes, *Army Group G: 10 May–22 September 1944* (B-800)
——, *German (OB Southwest) Estimate of Situation Prior to Allied Invasion of
      Southern France* (B-421)
Botsch, Walter, *Nineteenth Army June 1943–15 September 1944* (B-515)
von Gyldenfeldt, Heinz, *Army Group G: May–September 1944* (B-440, B-488,
      B-522, B-588, B-589)
Ruhfus, Heinrich, *Toulon Naval Commander 21 April–28 August 1944* (B-556)
Schramm, P. E., *OKW War Diary: 1 April–18 December 1944: The West* (B-034)
Schulz, Fritz, *Nineteenth Army 15 August–15 September 1944* (B-514)
von Sodenstern, Georg, *Southern France: Preparations for Invasion* (B-276)
——, *Nineteenth Army June 1943–15 September 1944, Commentary on B-515*
      (B-516)

Theisen, Edgar, *War History Reports—Activity of the Staff of Army Group G: 1 May–26 August 1944* (A-949)

Ullersperger, Wilhelm, *Nineteenth Army Fortress Engineer 1943–August 1944* (B-449)

Vogel, Walter, *Nineteenth Army Artillery: 4 April–18 August 1944* (B-575)

von Wietersheim, W., *The 11th Panzer Division in Southern France: 15 August–14 September 1944* (A-880)

Books

Adelman, Robert, and George Walton, *The Champagne Campaign* (Little, Brown, 1969)

Brager, Bruce, *The Texas 36th Division—A History* (Eakin: 2002)

Champeux, A., et P. Gaujac (ed.), *Le débarquement de Provence* (Lavauzelle: 2008)

Chazette, Alain, *L'Armée Allemande sur la Côte Méditerranéenne: AOK 19 Mittelmeerküstenfront* (Histoire & Fortifications: 2004)

——, *Atlantikwall-Südwall* (Histoire & Fortifications: 2004)

Jeffrey Clarke and Robert Smith, *The US Army in World War II: Riviera to the Rhine* (US Army Center for Military History: 1991)

Clayton, Anthony, *Three Marshals of France: Leadership after Trauma* (Brassey's: 1992)

Francois, D., and H. Julien, *Operation Dragoon: Le Débarquement de Provence 15 aôut 1944* (Cheminements: 2007)

Craven, Wesley, and James Cate, *The Army Air Forces in World War II*, Vol. 3 (Office of Air Force History: 1983)

Funk, Arthur, *Hidden Ally: The French Resistance, Special Operations, and the Landings in Southern France, 1944* (Greenwood: 1992)

Gaujac, Paul, *L'Armée de la Victoire de la Provence à l'Alsace 1944* (Lavauzelle: 1985)

——, *La battaille et la libération de Toulon* (Nouvelles Éditions Latines: 1994)

——, *Dragoon: The Other Invasion of France* (Histoire & Collections: 2004)

——, *La guerre en Provence 1944–45: une bataille méconnue* (Presses Universitaires de Lyon: 1998)

Giziowski, Richard, *The Enigma of General Blaskowitz* (Hippocrene: 1997)

Guiral, Pierre, *Libération de Marseille* (Hachette: 1974)

Hinsley, F. H., et. al., *British Intelligence in the Second World War*, Vol. 3, Part 2 (HMSO: 1988)

de Lattre, Jean, *The History of the French First Army* (Allen & Unwin: 1952)

Morison, Samuel, *The US Naval Operations in World War II: The Invasion of France and Germany 1944–45* (Little, Brown: 1957)

Robichon, Jacques, *The Second D-Day*, (Walker: 1962)

Ross, Robert, *The Supercommandos: 1st Special Service Force 1942–44* (Schiffer: 2000)

Taggart, Donald, *History of the Third Infantry Division in World War II* (Infantry Journal: 1947)

Tomblin, Barbara, *With Utmost Spirit: Allied Naval Operations in the Mediterranean 1942–1945* (Univ. Press of Kentucky: 2004)

Truscott, Lucian, *Command Missions: A Personal Story* (Presidio: 1990)

Wilt, Alan, *The French Riviera Campaign of August 1944* (S. Illinois University: 1982)

Volpe, Michael, *Task Force Butler: A Case Study in the Employment of an Ad Hoc Unit in Combat Operations* (US CGSC: 2007)

Yeide, Harry, and Mark Stout, *First to the Rhine: The 6th Army Group in World War II* (Zenith: 2007)

INDEX

Figures in **bold** refer to illustrations.